Imam al-Ghazali
The Book of Knowledge for Children

For the Prophet Muhammad ﷺ
and
his family
we humbly dedicate this effort.

Imam al-Ghazali
The Book of Knowledge
for Children
Book One from the
Ihya Ulum al-Din
The Revival of Religious Sciences

FONS VITAE

The Book of Knowledge For Children

*For Zainab, Maryam, Yusuf, Qasim, Abdullah
and Abdal Fattah*

First published in 2016 by
Fons Vitae
49 Mockingbird Valley Drive
Louisville, KY 40207
http://www.fonsvitae.com
Email: fonsvitaeky@aol.com

© 2016 Fons Vitae
No part of this book may be reproduced
in any form without prior permission of
the publishers. All rights reserved.

Library of Congress Control Number: 2015956967

ISBN 978-1941610-176

Printed in China

Illustrations by Clare C. Hagan
Thanks also to Aramco World and Mary Minifie
Cover by Michael Grimsdale
Endpapers by Mariam Yasin

Please frequent www.ghazalichildren.org for updates,
competitions, meeting one another and much more.

The decorative tree motif, found upon a carved panel in Nishapur, dates from the 11th or 12th century when Imam al-Ghazali studied in that Persian city, as does the included geometric ceramic ornament.

Table of Contents

Overview for Parents and Teachers	7
A Word from the Publisher	9
Introduction by Hamza Yusuf Hanson	11
Chapter 1 Two Kinds of Learning	23
Chapter 2 Animals and People	29
Chapter 3 The Two Worlds	33
Chapter 4 How to Enter the Garden	37
Chapter 5 Excellence of Learning	41
Chapter 6 The Best Gift of All	45
Chapter 7 How Do You Stay Really Happy All the Time?	49
Chapter 8 Pretend You Are a Tiny Seed	53
Chapter 9 The Three Things We Need Most in This Life	57
Chapter 10 Sharing the Treasure	63
Chapter 11 What Are Things You Must Learn	67
Chapter 12 Where Do the Wonderful Things We Can Learn Come From?	71
Chapter 13 More About the Two Worlds: A Family Trip	75
Chapter 14 Two Kinds of Things You Can Learn—Knowledge That Makes Your Heart Shine	83
Chapter 15 The Story of the Two Wolves	89
Chapter 16 Important Things You Cannot See	93
Chapter 17 More Ways to Make Your Heart Shine! and The Four Imams	97
Chapter 18 The Ant and the Pen	103

Chapter 19 A Little Boy Loses His Father's Horse	109
Chapter 20 The Little Gardens Inside the Garden	115
Chapter 21 How Can You Watch Your Very Own Hearts?	119
Chapter 22 Envy	123
Chapter 23 Having Pride and Being Spiteful	127
Chapter 24 Back-Biting	131
Chapter 25 Beware of Making Excuses, Bragging, Prying and Spying	135
Chapter 26 Not Wanting the Best for Others	139
Chapter 27 Being Two-Faced: Hypocrisy	143
Chapter 28 More Problems with Arguing	147
Chapter 29 A Question for You	151
Chapter 30 Your Heart Is Like a House	157
Chapter 31 Doing Too Many Things	161
Chapter 32 The Teacher, the Lion, and the Jug of Water	165
Chapter 33 When You Shoot an Arrow, You Need a Target	171
Chapter 34 The Camels Leave	177
Chapter 35 Grandfather Explains Some Important Ideas	183
Chapter 36 The Three Selves	187
Chapter 37 Getting Rich and Getting Knowledge	195
Chapter 38 Being a Teacher	201
Chapter 39 Playing School	205
Chapter 40 The Two Trees	209
Index of Sources	212

Overview for Parents and Teachers

Although al-Ghazali's *Book of Knowledge* was directed at a community of theologians, jurisprudents, and scholars, Fons Vitae found his insightful counsels could be usefully adapted for all ages.

The stories in this series are written for older children, but our intention is that parents and teachers read each one and then convey the ideas in such a way that it is clear to a child yet unable to read. Examples of how to do this are to be found on the accompanying instructional DVD. Many exercises in the workbooks are designed for small children with guidance from their family. The workbooks also contain material for older children, as well as activities and a curriculum to help reinforce Imam al-Ghazali's teachings in a practical way.

Please frequent our interactive website: <u>ghazalichildren.org</u>, where children may meet their global brothers and sisters and work together to create a better world. Essay and art competitions will be announced and submissions displayed. A section for parents and teachers invites contributions for further activities and reflections. Useful curriculum updates will regularly be provided. The Series' books can also be downloaded on this new website where a variety of other resources may be enjoyed as well.

Certain themes from al-Ghazali's Book One are presented repeatedly in the children's stories in order to emphasize their importance and underscore their urgency. Among them are:

—Divisions of Knowledge, its importance and sacred sources.
—The brevity of human life whose true purpose is to know and worship Allah ﷻ and prepare to meet Him.
—The Two Worlds: The fleeting enjoyment of this world and the Eternal Peace in the Abode of Permanence.
—Human dependence on God ﷻ, trust in His Will.
—The polishing of the Spiritual Heart: self-observation and correction, key virtues and harmful vices.
—The provisions and focus for life's journey, the importance of not wasting time.
—The quality of the true teacher and responsibility of the student: we are all teachers.
—Putting knowledge into practice.

Fons Vitae asks your forgiveness for any inaccuracies in our adaptation of Imam al-Ghazali's *Ihya* for the young. Please let us know of any mistakes that you might find so that future editions and the e-books may be corrected.

A Word from the Publisher

Dear Children,

You are about to read the wonderful *Book of Knowledge*, which offers some of the key ideas of the great Imam al-Ghazali, whose life story is to be found in the accompanying workbook.

In his writings, the Imam uses many stories and wonderful ideas that make his thoughts clear and exciting. If you are not able to read just yet, your parents and teachers will be delighted to tell you these stories in a way that is suited for your age and help you to answer many of the questions in the workbook, as well as enjoy the related activities. There is something for every age!

The many points that Imam al-Ghazali has gathered in the first of the 40 books of his *Ihya*, which is another name for *The Revival of the Religious Sciences*, are very important because they are like a summary of what the Imam teaches. Some of these ideas may be difficult to understand, but are made clear by the many stories taken from al-Ghazali. Sometimes, to help make a point clear, we have brought in stories from other cultures or traditions, such as the American Indians, the Japanese, and Central Asia. The Prophet Muhammad ﷺ told us that we should "seek knowledge even if from China."

Originally, this book was illustrated with drawings of imaginary children, but it was decided that this book is so important and serious that it would be better to give you pictures of real children who live throughout the Muslim world. In this way, you can meet your global brothers and sisters from Africa, Asia, the Middle East, and even North America.

As you already know, some words can have two meanings. And you will see what fun it can be learning to look for the secret meanings of words you already know. Let us take gold for example. You know that it is a beautiful metal which people use for money and decoration as well as jewelry. But if we say, "My mother has a heart of gold," or "That little boy is as good as gold," what could we also be saying? Perhaps you have learned that gold is the purest of all the metals because it can never tarnish or rust like other metals. It is also very soft and can easily be changed into other forms. It beautifully reflects light. You can see from the qualities of gold why we can use that word to describe a person's good heart. In the end we all want to keep our "hearts of gold." Imam al-Ghazali will tell us *how*.

The good heart must not tarnish or get dirty. It can change its ways to do something more beautifully. Also, this special *spiritual* heart reflects God's ﷻ light. Sometimes when we meet others they seem to be shining. In Arabic, a really good person is spoken of as *munawwar*—meaning lit up and not gloomy.

And of course the word "heart" has two meanings that you already know about. You have a heart inside you that beats and sends blood throughout your entire body. It is the center of life for humans. You can lose every other part of your body, including your brain, and still be alive if your heart is beating. The heart is the center. Like the sun it sends out life-giving energy. When we speak to each other "from the heart," we are not talking about the physical heart that pumps blood, but our spiritual hearts. The books of Imam al-Ghazali provide us with a special map which we can all follow in order to become our true, shining selves.

We very much hope you enjoy the *Book of Knowledge*.

Introduction
by Hamza Yusuf Hanson

Imam al-Ghazali is known as the "Proof of Islam." What is a proof? And why would the Muslim religion need a proof when we know our religion is true?

A proof tells us whether or not something really is what it says it is. You can prove or disprove a scientific theory by testing it to see if it is true or not. For example, scientists say that water freezes at 32 degrees Fahrenheit. If you want to find out if what they say is true, you can test it by doing your own experiment: You can place water in temperatures that get increasingly colder and colder and check with a thermometer to see if the water eventually freezes at 32 degrees Fahrenheit. If it does, then you have proved what the scientists claim.

Now that you know what it means to prove something, what do you think Muslim scholars meant when they called Imam al-Ghazali the "Proof of Islam"?

What the scholars meant when they called Imam al-Ghazali the "Proof of Islam" was simply that he had tested the practices in Islam and proved for himself that they were true. In other words, those practices had the effects that the Quran said they would have for people who practiced the commands of the Quran. For example, if you believe in God, then God will be enough proof for you. If you pray, and if your prayers are reasonable, sooner or later they will be answered. "Reasonable" here means that we can ask only for things that are possible: for example, we can't ask God to let us fly without an airplane or without some other material means to do so as that would be unreasonable.

Imam al-Ghazali "tested" the religion and proved that it does indeed do what it claims to do. He wrote a collection of 40 great books to help others to also "prove" Islam for themselves. He called that series of books *The Revival of Islamic Sciences*. "Revival" is the act of bringing something back to life. Imam al-Ghazali used this word because he thought that some Muslims had killed the spirit of Islam. What is the spirit of Islam? Spirit is what gives life to something, and what gives life to Islam is sincerity.

Imam Ibn Ata 'Illah, a great scholar from Egypt, said, "Actions are like bodies, and the spirit that brings those bodies to life is the sincerity with which they are done." He meant that when we do something without being sincere, or with ulterior motives, then that thing has no life and may as well be dead. For instance, if you give charity because you want people to think you are a generous person and not because it is the right thing to do, then you are not being sincere in giving charity. In that case, your motive or a reason only appears to be for charity but is really for a selfish purpose.

The word *charity* comes from a Latin word *caritas*, which means love. So charity should come from loving others and not from a desire to get something for yourself from the act. Imam al-Ghazali felt that many Muslims had lost the real reason for all of the practices we perform in our faith and that too many Muslims were doing them for the wrong reasons. So he wrote this great series of 40 books to show Muslims what the real reasons were for God's ﷻ sending a prophet with the teachings found in the Quran.

Imam al-Ghazali also planned his 40 books in a logical manner.

Introduction

He loved the science of logic. Logic teaches us how to think properly and avoid mistakes in our thinking. Because Imam al-Ghazali loved logic so much, he wrote his books logically. He went from one subject to another in a way that made sense, and this is very helpful to us when we read what he wrote. In fact, he divided this great work of his into 40 small books because it is easier for us to learn smaller chunks of information. The reason he chose 40 is because 40 is a special number.

There are other special numbers. For instance, did you ever notice that you have ten fingers? Did you also notice that all numbers are made from ten digits? We call this "base ten." The ten digits are from one to nine and zero. When we write two digits, the number one and then zero, we get the number ten. In fact, all our numbers come from just these ten digits: one through nine and zero!

Forty is a special number, like one, three, five, and seven, which are also special. Forty is special because God told Moses, the main prophet of the Hebrew bible, peace be upon him, that he would have 40 days and nights to prepare for his meeting with God. So Moses worked very hard praying and fasting for 40 days and nights before he went to Mount Sinai to meet with God. Now this doesn't mean that God was in a place. God cannot be in a place because God is uncreated, and God created all places. So it means that God is everywhere in His knowledge: that is to say, God knows about everything that is going on in every place. So Moses had a spiritual (not physical) meeting with God on Mount Sinai.

When Imam al-Ghazali wrote his work, he thought long and hard about the most important and unique possession that human beings have. He realized that what makes us different is that unlike all other animals, we can *think*, and we can use language to communicate what we think in ways that no animal can. So he concluded that knowledge is the most important thing. This is why he begins his work with the *Book of Knowledge*. In it, Imam al-Ghazali tells us what knowledge is and why it is important. He also tells us about the pitfalls or dangers of knowledge. Some people use knowledge for the wrong reasons. For instance, knowledge of airplanes can be used for good or bad purposes. We can use an airplane to take people over great distances in a short time, and that is something good that knowledge of airplanes enables us to do. But we can also use that same knowledge of airplanes to cruelly drop bombs on people who are different from us and with whom we may disagree.

Imam al-Ghazali then went on to write the *Book of Creed*. *Creed* is what you believe, and he wanted people to believe the correct things about God. So in that book, he talked about the six things every Muslim must truly believe and why. Then he wrote about each of the five pillars of Islam in his next five books. Do you know the five pillars and why they are called "pillars"? One of the pillars is the prayer, and the prayer is done five times a day. So there are five pillars, and Muslims have to pray five times a day. Five is one of the special numbers!

Did you know that all numbers are either even or odd? Any number you can think of is either even or odd. For example, the number 24 is an even number. Why is it even? It is even because you can split it perfectly in half. Half of 24 is 12, which is also an even number. You can split 12 in half, which is six. But an odd number can never be split in half without using a fraction. (Fractions are also written using the ten digits.) Five is an odd number. Five is the first number that is the sum of the first even and odd numbers, two and three.

Introduction

Did you know that in Arabic, *one* is not considered a number on its own but only as part of all numbers? For example, the number two is made of two ones, the number three comprises three ones, and so on. All numbers begin with one because all things came from one source. That source is The One (*al-Wahid*), which is a name of God. Another amazing fact about one is that the world is made up of elements, and every element in the world has a mass, and the element that is most widespread in the universe is Hydrogen. Three-fourths of the universe, in other words 75 out of every 100 of the elements in the universe, is made up of Hydrogen. Guess what the atomic number of Hydrogen is? It is one!

In addition to prayer, Imam al-Ghazali also wrote about the other four pillars. These five Muslim practices are called pillars because they hold up the faith like pillars hold up a house. The 20th book Imam al-Ghazali wrote is about the character or behavior of the Prophet Muhammad, God's peace and blessings upon him. Why do you think Imam al-Ghazali made that book number 20? He did that because 20 is exactly half of 40, so the "heart" or center of his work is about the Prophet, God's peace and blessings upon him. The Prophet, God's peace and blessings upon him, is the heart of Islam, so Imam al-Ghazali made the book that is about the Prophet, God's peace be upon him, the heart of the whole work.

Can you guess what the last book of his work is called? It is *The Book of Death and the Afterlife*. He made this the last book because just as Moses was given 40 days and nights to prepare for meeting with God, Imam al-Ghazali gave us 40 books to help us prepare for death, when we will also meet God.

Death is the end of life, but it is also a beginning. When we die, we go back to our source. We came from another world, and the Prophet, God's peace and blessings upon him, said, "Be in the world like a stranger or a traveler who stops to take shade under a tree and then move on." We are here on this earth for only a short time, and we have been brought here to learn as much as we can about why we are here, what we should do while we are here, and how to prepare for where we go when we leave here. Imam al-Ghazali wrote his work of 40 books to explain these things to us. He loved us so much that he wanted to help us reach our goal safely and to be ready for the next stage of our journey back to our source.

When Imam al-Ghazali was very young, he had a great desire to learn. He studied almost all the time, and his teachers were amazed at how hard he worked to understand his subjects. As he grew, he became very skilled at debating. The art of how to argue and persuade others is called *debate*. He could debate anyone about any subject, and he was so learned and persuasive that he would always win. Soon he became a great scholar of many subjects, such as Arabic, Persian, logic, and grammar, and he excelled especially in the subject of law.

Imam al-Ghazali was one of the greatest lawyers in Muslim history. A lawyer studies law to protect it from being abused or used wrongly. Some lawyers defend people accused of crimes while others prosecute or argue against the person accused of a crime. Imam al-Ghazali didn't defend or prosecute people. He was the kind of lawyer who wrote about what law is and how it works. In other words, he was a philosopher of law.

The word *philosophy* means "love of wisdom" and comes from two Greek words, *philo* (love) and *sophos* (wisdom). So a true philosopher is someone who loves wisdom. Do you know what wisdom is? It is using our knowledge in the best way possible. For example, sometimes, the best thing to do

Introduction

is be silent and other times, the best thing to do is speak up. Wisdom tells us when we should be silent and when we should speak up. Good laws are wise laws. In other words, they contain wisdom. So even knowing when to apply a law, or not, is part of law. For example, stealing is wrong. But if a person is starving, and no one will give him any food, then God will not punish such a person for taking what he needs to survive. But it is only a wise person who can determine when stealing is punishable or not punishable: that is, only a wise person can decide that someone who steals deserves punishment or that he should not be punished because he was under duress or great difficulty. So laws need wise people to understand how to apply them but also when they should not be applied. This is the aspect of law that Imam al-Ghazali wrote about. He was one of wisest lawyers in history.

Imam al-Ghazali had a great teacher named Imam al-Juwayni. He taught Imam al-Ghazali that all of Islamic law has five reasons behind it: the first one is to protect your religion; the second is to protect your life; the third is to protect your mind; the fourth is to protect your wealth and property; and the fifth is to protect your family.

Later on, another great scholar realized one more universal principle was missing and added a sixth one, which is to protect your dignity. Do you know what dignity is? It is what makes you a special creature and why you should always behave in ways that honor and protect your special place with God. God did not make you like a snake that slithers and slides on its belly, or like a dog that walks on all fours. Instead, God made you a creature that walks upright. Upright means straight, not bent or crooked. It also has a second meaning, which is to behave in a good way, with virtue and excellence. So dignity is something every human being has, but some lose it or let others take it from them. Sometimes, bad people purposely degrade or humiliate others: that means they take their dignity from them. For instance, some people will treat others badly because their skin color is different. In Islam, that is wrong because it goes against this sixth reason behind Islamic law, which is to protect dignity. The Quran says that it is a sign of God when we see people with complexions of different colors. So when you see a red, black, yellow, or white person, you should be amazed that God made so many different colors of skin!

Imam al-Ghazali wrote a lot about law and why it is so important: laws help us live together in peace. When we don't have laws or when some people break laws, they harm others or take their property or even kill them! These are all wrong, and laws prevent people from doing the wrong things. But once in a while, some people do the wrong things anyway, and laws punish them for two reasons: the first is so that they won't be punished in the Next World, and the second is so that others won't do the same things in this world by imitating them, in other words, by copying their bad behavior. Humans like to copy others, and that is why we should look for good and saintly people to copy and not bad and devilish people.

When Imam al-Ghazali became a great scholar, the ruler made him the head of the greatest university in the world in Baghdad, Iraq. Imam al-Ghazali was only 30 years old at that time, and some people were jealous of him because he was so wise and knowledgeable at such a young age. But Imam al-Ghazali would just debate them and make them look bad by showing how he was right and they were wrong. He did this often. But then he realized that he wasn't being very nice. He started to feel like a show off because he enjoyed it when

Introduction

people praised him for being so smart.

Deep down, Imam al-Ghazali knew that he was better than someone who enjoyed hearing his own praise, and he wanted to meet his better self. He knew that we all have three selves living inside us. These are called the commanding self, the blaming self, and the peaceful self. The commanding self is our lowest self. It is selfish and wants everything for itself. It doesn't like to share or help others. Some people let it dominate the other two selves, and they become horrible people. But the second self, the blaming self, is a better self because it doesn't like the lowest self and blames it for doing bad things. Do you know how sometimes you might get angry at your mother and say something mean to her, but later you feel bad and ask yourself, "Why did I do that?" The answer is that first self made you do that, which is why it is called the commanding self. And the second self knows that was wrong and makes you feel bad: that is why it is called the blaming self. Imam al-Ghazali knew that he had to fight his lowest self. So when he did something wrong, he would punish his lowest self by fasting or giving charity until he stopped doing wrong things.

Once he conquered his lowest self, Imam al-Ghazali didn't need to blame himself anymore, and his true self came out: this is called the self at peace or the peaceful soul. This is who we *really are*, but it takes a long time for us to become that person. The 40 books Imam al-Ghazali wrote are like a map that we can follow for the journey to become our true selves. He made the journey and proved that if any of us took the same journey, it would take us to the same place. That place is called Paradise. He was proving for himself what the Prophet Muhammad, God's peace and blessings upon him, told us, and, in this way, he would have no doubts that he was giving us sound knowledge that he himself had learned through practice. Imam al-Ghazali showed that others who follow his 40 books would undertake that same journey and also prove for themselves that the practices of Islam were true, and find their peaceful souls and no longer do things that harmed their souls.

The Quran tells us not to harm our souls, but God also says, in a chapter called, "The Spider" that those who "fight [against themselves] in Our way, We will guide them to Our paths" (Q 29:69). God uses the plural "We" because God is great. When God says "We," that is a special "we": it is called "the royal We." Also, when God says "fight" here, it means "struggle" because this verse was sent down when the Prophet, God's peace and blessings upon him, was in Mecca, and he was not allowed to defend himself if someone attacked him while he was in Mecca. So the fighting in this verse actually means to struggle with the lower self. God promises that if we do that, He will guide us to the special paths of wisdom, so we will always know which path to go down when different circumstances arise. A circumstance is a situation or condition you find yourself in. Life has many different situations, and in each one, we need wisdom so that we can choose to do the right thing.

You have a precious soul that God has placed within your body in a way that makes you unique. That means no one else is like you. When you came into this world through your mother's womb or tummy, you were pure, like gold or snow. But you had this lower self in you that pretends to be the real you. When you fight that false self, your true self begins to shine. This is why we say about some people that they are full of light. Imam al-Ghazali wrote this book so that you could shine brightly in

Introduction

a dark world and be a light for others. When you follow his teaching, which is really following the Prophet Muhammad's teaching, which is really following God's teaching, you will shine, and others will see that light, and some will want you to show them how they can get that light too; still others will want to steal it from you because it is so precious. But Imam al-Ghazali's 40 books will teach you how to make your light shine brightly and also how to protect it by bringing to life the sciences of our faith.

I hope you learn all the things in these 40 books one day and use the whole work as a map for your life. It has everything you need to find your true self, your bright, shining self.

The Book of Knowledge For Children

Did you know that there is one book wherein you will find all the knowledge you need to take care of your invisible, spiritual Heart?

Chapter 1
Two Kinds of Learning

The children were all talking at once. Their days were filled with school and prayer, so much of the conversation centered around those subjects. Some began to talk among themselves about what they were learning. They found that they shared many of the same questions and concerns. After some searching, behind a stone wall of a forgotten garden in the neighborhood, they discovered a quiet hidden spot that they decided to make into a secret meeting place. In that meeting place they could gather and talk about what worried them.

At the first meeting Ahmad confided, "My parents are really upset if I miss any of my prayers. I am too shy to ask them why we really have to pray."

Layla chimed in, "And I don't understand why we are asked to do so many things in our religion. I don't understand the *real* meaning of what we are supposed to do. I am not even sure why we really need to learn the Quran."

"I have an idea," said Maryam. "Haven't we all noticed that beautiful elderly man who seems to be always sitting silently on a park bench in the sun? When our parents and grandparents pass by him, they always nod toward him with respect, placing their right hands over their hearts. I have even heard my mother say that he is radiant, which I think means something like *glowing*."

"Oh yes!" added Yusuf. "Even the birds come very near to him, and he greets them. The birds seem to love him, too."

Qasim suggested, "Why don't we go together right this minute to see if he is in the park? He seems to be very kind and wise. Perhaps we could ask him if he would come to our secret meeting place and help us with our questions."

To the great delight of the children this lovely older gentleman agreed and accompanied them to their hidden spot in the forgotten garden of the town. Yusuf noticed a tree stump covered with soft moss and offered it as a seat to their new friend.

The children introduced themselves, after which their kind new teacher added, "Please call me Haj Abdullah."

Qasim asked, "So you have made the Haj pilgrimage, sir?"

Haj Abdullah spoke very softly, "My dear children, we are *all* on a pilgrimage together in this life, returning ultimately to our Creator. Let us begin now with your questions. But let us start with what *learning* is itself!"

The children groaned.

"Not more school!" Maryam whispered under her breath.

"I heard that!" noted the smiling elder. "Not all learning has to be boring." He cleared his throat and said a little louder, "This afternoon we will start with what learning actually *is*!"

This time no one complained. If Haj Abdullah were anything, it was clear to them that he was not boring. And so he began.

"Children, sometimes your mother and father teach you useful things such as how to take care of yourself. They say, 'Don't run too fast, you might fall and hurt yourself.' 'Look both ways before you cross the street in case a car is coming!' 'This is the way you brush your teeth correctly, the way to take care of them! Don't eat too many sweets!' This kind of learning is protecting your *body* from harm.

"From our parents we learn about love and family values. Our parents also instruct us with practical wisdom, so that we may grow up to be healthy, safe, and sound."

The children nodded in agreement. They knew this.

The elder continued, "Life is a blessed chance to learn! In school we learn subjects like math and reading. The knowledge learned at home and school helps you take care of your mind and body. But did you know that there is another special kind of learning, a *higher,* more real learning that takes care of your heart? We actually have a rich tradition full of this higher learning. While there have been many great teachers of the heart, one of the best teachers was Imam al-Ghazali, whom you have heard about from your parents and teachers. So let us learn from the great master of the heart!"

The children now had new questions and were a bit confused. How could their hearts need to learn anything?

Their new friend explained, "Imam al-Ghazali teaches us that inside us we actually have two hearts. The first heart, the physical heart, pumps blood throughout the body. The second heart, however, is invisible. You cannot see it. This heart is your *spiritual* heart, and just like your physical heart, your spiritual heart needs great care and love. Your parents help you care for this special heart by reminding you to be good. Perhaps your mother reminds you to be gentle with the cat or to share your toys." Everyone nodded. Sharing was a problem.

He continued, "Did you know that there is one book wherein you will find all the knowledge you need for taking care of this invisible, spiritual heart? That book is the Quran, the very words of Allah ﷻ that were revealed to us through the Prophet Muhammad ﷺ. The Quran teaches us about that special learning, that higher learning that protects our spiritual hearts and makes them strong! And when we make our spiritual hearts better, we prepare ourselves for Paradise, a kind of garden that is *so* beautiful you can't even imagine it. It's like this world, only much, much better!

"Can you give examples of these two kinds of learning in your life now? What have you been learning to keep your *body* safe? What has your *heart* been learning?" Haj Abdullah called on Layla.

"I have been learning to brush my hair and put it into braids all by myself!" she said.

The children's new teacher persisted, "Is that the only reason you brush your hair?"

"Well . . ." she thought for a moment, "I don't want to let any birds think it's a good place to build a nest!"

Haj Abdullah laughed gently. Later he would explain to them that even when practical learning is done with true understanding, it leads to the higher learning of the heart. "Good enough. Now what has your heart been learning?"

Zainab, who had said nothing up to this point, raised her hand. "My heart has learned that it makes my mother happy when I help her with my younger brothers and sisters. Especially at bedtime."

"Now that is a good heart lesson: to be kind to one's parents who give so much to you already. Anyone else?" asked their new friend.

Layla raised her hand. The old man nodded toward her. "My heart learned to be happy for my friend when she got a new dolly, even though I really wanted a new dolly, too."

Haj Abdullah smiled and his face shone with contentment. "Another good lesson for the heart. What time shall we meet tomorrow?"

The children were greatly relieved. They had so many questions about life. And here was a beautiful, kind, and peaceful man who was going to help them find some answers.

The Book of Knowledge For Children

How could people be better than animals?

Chapter 2
Animals and People

At the agreed upon hour Haj Abdullah met with the neighborhood children in the secret meeting place. As he approached, he noticed the children chasing after a little rabbit that was scurrying between the bushes.

As everyone gathered around him, their new friend asked, "Can you guess why human beings are better than animals? How can this be so? Isn't the elephant much bigger? Isn't the camel, who can carry heavy loads for long distances, much stronger than you? Is not the fierce lion bolder and braver than you? If all these facts are true, in what way can human beings be better than animals?"

The children were silent.

"Did you know that only humans have special, *spiritual* hearts. Only *we* can learn ways to be close to Allah ﷻ and be loved by Him. What is important is what we *know,* not how big or strong we are, but that we use our spiritual hearts. Just as our bodies need food, our hearts need food, too. Think about the kinds of food your body needs. Now think about what you are feeding your heart."

Layla, who had been listening carefully, answered, "I am eating lots of fruits and vegetables for my body."

"But an animal can do that as well," Haj Abdullah pointed out. "What makes you better?"

"I can cook the fruits into a pie!" said Layla. "No animal can do that!"

"True. But be serious. Tell me about your heart. What have you learned lately for your spiritual heart?"

"For my heart, I listen carefully to my family and teacher who are showing me how to be very kind, and are teaching me what Allah ﷻ wants most of all for us," replied Layla.

"And what is that?" asked the wise friend.

Layla said nothing. She waited for their new friend and teacher to answer his own question. But instead, he stood up as he watched Qasim, who looked pale and frightened, running towards him.

Imam al-Ghazali

The Book of Knowledge For Children

When you look around you see the beautiful world God ﷻ made, full of trees and birds, green grass and mountains, lit by the golden sun and silver moon! Did you know that after we die, there is another more beautiful world called Paradise?

Chapter 3
The Two Worlds

Qasim ran up to the wise teacher who was now standing beneath a flowering tree under a beautiful afternoon sky. Qasim was very upset.

"Dear Teacher, quick! Come over here! There is a tiny baby bird which must have fallen out of its nest, and it is dead!"

Haj Abdullah placed his hand tenderly on Qasim's shoulder. "My son, there are two worlds you must be aware of. This one that we are in *now* is very brief and has many problems. Allah ﷻ promises all of us that we will experience loss in three ways. We will not have some of our expectations fulfilled as we had hoped. Besides loss of these hopes and dreams, we and those we love will lose our good health. And finally we will all lose our lives on *this* earth. But then we will continue on to the next truly magnificent and glorious world that lasts forever and is a place where there are no longer any problems."

The children now moved in more closely toward their dignified friend. Everyone wanted to know about the *two* worlds. They listened attentively.

Haj Abdullah began, "When you look around, you see the beautiful world God ﷻ made, full of trees and birds, green grass and mountains, lit by the golden sun and silver moon. Did you know that after we die, there is another more beautiful world called Paradise or Heaven? But in order to reach Heaven, we have to make preparations. Heaven, the best of all life's rewards, is for those who prepare. And we get ready for Heaven by making our invisible hearts stronger and better, and we strengthen our spiritual hearts by doing what is right and learning what is true. If you are going on a trip, don't you prepare? That is what Allah ﷻ, Who has made us, has asked us to do. And aren't we fortunate that God ﷻ sent the Angel Gabriel to our Prophet Muhammad ﷺ and revealed to him all of the things that we need to learn and do, to get ready?"

The children were silent. This was important to understand.

"Did you know that when you recite words from the Quran, you are saying the very same words the Angel Gabriel said to our beloved Prophet Muhammad? ﷺ Just imagine! When you say or recite from the Quran you are actually saying the same words that the Angel Gabriel revealed! And these words, sent from Allah ﷻ, tell us how to be really good and how to get to the Garden of Paradise when we have finished living our lives on this earth."

The children could immediately see why getting to repeat the verses of the Quran was amazing!

Haj Abdullah paused. "Let me tell you a story. There was a wonderful man named Hasan al-Basri who lived in Medina after the Prophet Muhammad ﷺ died and went on to Paradise. Someone asked Hasan what these words of the Quran mean: 'Our Lord, give us goodness in this world and goodness in the Next World.' He explained, 'Goodness in this world is knowledge, and goodness in the Next World is Heaven.' So my children, what did Hasan al-Basri mean?" inquired Haj Abdullah.

"That the best thing in this world is Real Learning, the learning that helps our hearts within us and teaches us how to worship God ﷻ and how to treat others kindly and beautifully. And if we have that knowledge, then when we finish our lives here, we will journey to Heaven where the Garden of Paradise awaits us. But how do we get there?" asked Qasim.

"Indeed, children. How *do* we get there?" repeated Haj Abdullah.

No one raised a hand. But they wanted to *know*.

The Book of Knowledge For Children

*What doesn't sink if your boat tips over?
What could swim with you?*

Chapter 4
How to Enter the Garden

Haj Abdullah repeated his question. "How can we be near to God ﷻ in *this* world and enter Heaven in the Next World? Not by simply getting a lot of things in this life, wanting more and more things, but instead by being beautiful inside our hearts.

"Imam al-Ghazali explained it this way. If you were in a boat that tipped over and then sank, all your toys would float away and sink to the bottom of the sea. The things we have in this world, our clothes or games or toys, never last. Our clothes, and even our bodies, get old and worn out; games and toys get broken or lost. But if we have a beautiful, shining, spiritual heart; it lasts forever. We can swim with it!

"What you have learned, and then the *way* you become as a person from what you have learned, can never be lost. You get to keep your spiritual heart knowledge forever and ever. So that is what you want to hold on to and keep strong! It is your shining heart that will get you into the Heavenly Garden. And Imam al-Ghazali can show you how to make your spiritual heart shine! And where you will find the hidden treasure."

The elder stood up. He seemed to look like a kind of king, even though his clothes were simple and he wore no crown. He gazed at the moon, which was just starting to rise in the sky. "Ah, the nighttime is coming. We will soon have to break for another day."

"No!" cried the children.

"Not yet!"

"We aren't done."

"We never heard what the Imam wanted us to know. About the hidden treasure!"

"Yes, that's true," said Haj Abdullah. "All right, just because I mentioned it before, I will continue."

The children sighed with great relief, and settled in more closely to listen.

Imam al-Ghazali

The Book of Knowledge For Children

The key to finding the treasure is asking questions.

Chapter 5
Excellence of Learning

Haj Abdullah waved his hands in the air. "Look at this treasure chest! Would you like to know what is inside of it?"

There was no real treasure chest in front of the children. But they listened as the elder drew a picture in the air with his words.

"Knowledge is similar to sealed storerooms. Inside are the precious jewels of learning and truth and great ideas. A kind of learning that is food to nourish your heart! But these storehouses are sealed shut! Oh dear! What sort of key will open the way in for you? The answer is simple. Anyone can find it. The key is wanting to know and asking questions! The key is learning and finding true knowledge. When you seek true learning and ask questions in order to know the truth, God ﷻ will give you goodness in return for your noble efforts, as well as to those who try their best to answer your questions. So every time you seek knowledge from your grandfather or teacher or mother and listen to the answers carefully—God ﷻ will reward *all* of you, and will Himself be pleased!"

"So if we ask questions all the time we will not get in trouble?" asked Yusuf.

"Indeed not!" stated Haj Abdullah. "Imagine your heart shining with knowledge. We *all* can be teachers. You," he pointed toward Amina, "can teach Layla, who can teach Zainab . . . It's like a chain. We all question together, and we learn together."

"So what my parents teach me, I should share with my friends?" asked Qasim.

"Yes! Precisely!" said Haj Abdullah. "Don't your mothers and fathers and teachers and grandparents teach you about being good and kind to others? Iman al-Ghazali mentions that the Prophet Muhammad ﷺ said that when you learn about some good thing to do and then do it yourself and then others *copy* you, this is one of the greatest things of all! Maybe your mother reminds you, 'That little girl in your class has no friends. So be her friend.' Then, when other children see you being friendly to her, they will want to copy you because they can see how really, really wonderful it is to be a friend to one who is friendless. Well, then find another good thing to *do* and teach it to others just by doing it yourself. If you do what you are taught, the angels in Paradise will be waiting for you."

Haj Abdullah rose. "It is now time to go back to your families. I will meet you here tomorrow after you have finished your studies and your chores." The children wondered where he lived; no one seemed to know.

They thanked the beloved elder and each went his or her own way, contemplating the beautiful bits of knowledge being imparted. Haj Abdullah always left them with something to think about—or more questions to ask at the next special gathering.

Imam al-Ghazali

The Book of Knowledge For Children

The Prophet ﷺ said that truly God's angels and those of His Heavens and His earth, even to the ant in its hill, and the fish in the sea, all ask God to bless the one who teaches people the path to goodness.

Chapter 6
The Best Gift of All

Haj Abdullah arrived early and was already waiting for them when they all arrived. "I have a story for you," he said. "It's about a little girl named Sara. Sara was nearly six years old. She loved her mother so much that she was forever making little drawings and other surprises for her. Her mother was truly delighted with all these darling presents Sara made.

"Then one day little Sara thought about how her parents and grandmother were often talking about ways we can have more beautiful hearts and how we can be more giving and generous. 'Look how generous Allah ﷻ is! He gives us the world, birds, trees, our families!' Sara's father said. Then he mentioned that Imam al-Ghazali reminds us that a most excellent gift is to pass on to others what we have learned. The best way to do that is to do that good thing ourselves, so that others will notice our example and do it too because it is so good. Sara heard her father add, 'The Prophet ﷺ said that 'Truly God's ﷻ angels and those of His Heavens and His earth, even to the ant in its hill, and the fish in the sea, ask God to bless the one who teaches people the path to goodness.'"

The children were all wide-eyed especially when Haj Abdullah added, "And Imam al-Ghazali reminds us that knowledge is the life of the heart. Wild and grazing animals, as well as the Heavens and the stars, ask forgiveness for such teachers."

The children were astounded. All of these wonderful and amazing things could happen if they simply acted beautifully and taught by example!

The elder paused, stroking his beard, his silvery hair catching the light of the late afternoon sun. He continued his story. "Sara thought to herself, *I could teach what I have been hearing and learning, and the best way would be to do it myself!* So she thought about a little girl named Selma, whom she noticed people ignored. Selma was very sad and lonely. Sara thought, *I, too, can be generous and giving! It's not that hard and would be fun to do!* She went to this lonely girl and became her real friend. She gave Selma some of her toys but most of all, she gave her what she needed most—a friend! And that little girl was so touched by this goodness that she wanted to do the same for another child! So Selma became the friend of *another* girl, Nadia, who was *also* in need of a friend. Sara's mother watched all of this and hugged her daughter, exclaiming, 'This is the *best* gift to me in all the world, that you learned about something good to do and did it yourself and inspired another little girl to do it too, like a chain of mercy! You are the best little girl in the world, and what you did is the most wonderful gift that your mother could ever want!'

"And do you know what else?" continued Haj Abdullah. "That night, the ants and fish in the sea and angels all prayed for Sara!" The neighborhood children all gasped.

"I want all the creatures to pray for me, too!" said Layla.

"Then think: What kinds of gifts like this can you think to give? Imam al-Ghazali is *your* teacher, too, along with your parents, grandparents, teachers at school, and even each other. He tells us that the Prophet ﷺ said that if you learn good things and then *do* them, which is like teaching others by *showing* them what to do, the angels will seek to be your close friends and will stroke you with their wings. So listen carefully and learn everything you can with joy!"

As if to explain what joy meant, their dear teacher began to quietly sing the most beautiful song, even the birds seemed to fall silent in the trees to listen. The children understood that this song was a sign of joy and that all they had to do to feel joy was to sing God's ﷻ praises as well. '*Al-hamdulilah*' they all chanted in unison. 'Praise the Lord.'"

It was time for Haj Abdullah to depart. He watched as little Layla skipped her way out of the secret meeting place. The children all went home to put what they were learning into action, just as their noble friend had encouraged them to.

The Book of Knowledge For Children

"If I win a game or get a new toy, I am happy for a short time. So what can keep me content all the time?"

Chapter 7
How Do You Stay Really Happy All the Time?

Layla got home well before dark. "Mommy," she said, "today I learned a fun way to express joy: through singing God's ﷻ praises!"

Little Layla's mother asked her, "Haven't you noticed that you can be happy in two ways? One way is when something happens to you like getting a new toy or doing things with your family. That makes you happy, doesn't it? But only for a little while! Do you stay happy all the time, hour after hour if you get a nice present or toy?"

"If I win a game or get a new toy, I am happy for a little while," Layla replied. "Yes, Mommy, it's true! So what can keep me happy *all* the time? I want to *always* be happy."

Mother explained. "True, lasting happiness is found only in your invisible heart for it is in this heart that we are near to Allah ﷻ and the angels! And how do we reach this heart? By doing what is right. For example, have you ever noticed that after you pray or help someone in need, that you feel a deep happiness? Did you know that you feel this deeper, greater happiness because you have made your invisible heart stronger, your true and beautiful spiritual heart!"

"Oh, yes," replied Layla. "I have noticed that happens."

Mother continued, "And remember, when you do what is right and beautiful, you become a good and beautiful person. After learning *how* to be good and then practicing that goodness, you are actually opening all the secret, special doors that will be taking you to the Heavenly Garden of Paradise. That's where, one day, you will be totally and completely and joyfully happy forever and ever!"

"Oh Mommy, I want to be in that beautiful garden with you and everyone I love, *always*. And *all* I have to do is learn the *special* and easy ways to be good. Wow! I can do that! Having fun with my toys is lovely, but sometimes, Mommy, I get tired of playing games. I am so glad the Quran teacher is teaching me how to get near to the angels and Allah ﷻ. How can anybody get tired of that? Now I *see* why teaching and learning about Allah ﷻ is the best, most real and true thing I can do!"

Layla spread her arms out wide to her parents. "Thank you, Mother and Father, for showing me and reminding me about what is really true! As you said, if I win a game or get a new toy, I am happy for a while. So what can keep us happy all the time? Now I know that by simply doing what I do every day in a new and special way, like when I help wash the dishes, instead of being *un*happy, I can change this into a way of making my special, true heart stronger. I can be joyful *all* the time. I will start by smiling at everyone!" With this Layla skipped off to bed. She understood how her very own life, just the way it was, was filled with ways she could use to polish her heart and be nearer to the angels.

Imam al-Ghazali

The Book of Knowledge For Children

Now, pretend you are one of those tiny, golden seeds you just planted!

Chapter 8
Pretend You Are a Tiny Seed

As a special surprise, Mother Haajar gave one of her sons, ten-year-old Abdullah, two small packets of seeds. One was for flowers, and one had seeds that could grow into large beautiful trees. She explained, "As you carefully plant these seeds, pretend that the ground is this world we live in now. As your flowers and little trees grow up tall into the sky, pretend that they are reaching with their branches, like little arms, up to Heaven!"

"Oh," said Abdullah, "that sounds like fun. I will make sure I find a good place in the garden with plenty of sun so they will be able to grow nicely."

"Abdullah, you are so bright and intelligent. Now pretend that *you* are one of those tiny seeds just planted in a warm earthen bed for seeds! What will you need to grow up to be tall and noble and beautiful?"

Abdullah replied, "Well, Mother, trees and flowers need water and sun to grow, but I am a boy. What I need in order to grow up to be tall and noble is Real Learning, the kind that will show me how to be close to the heavens and angels."

Abdullah's mother nodded, and said, "Yes, this world is only where we are living now, just for the time being. Imam al-Ghazali compared it to fields and seedbeds where things are planted and have a chance to grow. This world gives us a chance to grow and have time to polish our golden hearts with good deeds."

"I want to grow up to be like a field of beautiful flowers, too!" cried Abdullah's little sister, Layla.

"Child, there is plenty of time for you to grow into a beautiful bed of flowers," said Haajar, "but for now we have to get you ready for bed."

Layla was too excited to go to sleep. She still had more questions. Abdullah sighed. He knew that questions were good, that they were part of learning, but sometimes his little sister seemed to never stop talking! But he knew that God ﷻ loves those who are patient with others.

Imam al-Ghazali

The Book of Knowledge For Children

"Well, the Imam said some people spend all their life just getting more and more, beyond what they really NEED and they have forgotten why they were born and even about how to get ready for the next life."

Chapter 9
The Three Things We Need Most in This Life

"Mother, I am starting to understand that I need to grow up like a beautiful field of flowers. I also am beginning to understand what kinds of things I need to learn in order to go to the Next World with you, Daddy, Abdullah, Bilal, Zainab, and everyone I love. But what about *this* world, our earth, where we live now? What do I need for *now*?"

"Oh, of course! This world! Well, Layla, first let me ask you what you need for sure, every day?"

"Let's see . . . food! Oh food! Yes! I'm even hungry now. When is dinner time?"

"Layla! You just finished lunch!" Mother commented. "Be serious. After food, the second thing you need most is clothing to keep you warm, to cover and to protect you from the sun and rain and snow."

Layla said, "And Mommy, we need to live somewhere! I need a bed to sleep in at night."

"Yes," Haajar answered. "Exactly, we need food *first*, the *second* need is clothes, and then the *next* most important thing we need is a home to shelter us from the hot weather, the rain, and the cold. Our home keeps us safe while we sleep! Now Layla, where do these three needed things come from?"

"Well, I have seen farmers growing fruits and vegetables which we then buy from a market. So the farmer and shopkeeper take money for getting our food to us, and they live from that

57

money. And then they buy what they need like clothes and houses, right?"

"Oh, Layla, you are such an bright little girl! I am so proud. And also, ask yourself where do clothes come from?"

"Coats can be made from wool, like my coat!" Layla exclaimed. "And I know wool comes from fluffy sheep! Where does cotton come from?"

Haajar explained, "Clothes can also be made from cotton which grows on the earth. The cotton plant has little pods. In each pod, we can find a tiny ball of white cotton."

"So you mean people pick the cotton balls and then make cloth from them?" asked Layla.

"Right!" said Mother. "And what about houses? Let's think what they are made of."

Layla thought about this, "Well, our house is made of bricks, wood, and glass for the windows."

Haajar was pleased. "Yes, and also some houses are of stone, some have metal, and in some places people make wonderful houses with mud."

"So, I see," said Layla. "Then someone makes a drawing of what kind of house or school they need, for other people who know how build it! I will draw the kind of house I would like when I am a mommy."

"But sadly, there is now a big problem, Layla, that Imam al-Ghazali tells us about. Allah ﷻ made us and put us to grow up and live in *this* world in order to have enough time to know and love and learn about Him, the One Who gave us everything, our lives and our families. But some people forget that we are here for just a short while in *this* world. They never learned how their true, invisible, special hearts can help them to become beautiful people, ready for the Next World. And do you know how they spend their whole lives? What they do all day long, every day?"

"No," said Layla, "what? I want to know, Mommy, to make sure I'm doing the right thing."

"Well, the Imam said some people spend all their lives just getting more and more of every sort of thing, beyond what they really need. They have forgotten why they were even born and even about how to get ready for the Next Life. They have forgotten both their beginning and their end."

"What do you mean, Mommy? What do they do with their lives all day long?"

"Well, remember that food is our first need? And we know that our Prophet Muhammad ﷺ said that the best people were careful to eat just what they really need to have healthy bodies. We try to give you fruits and fresh vegetables to eat so that you will not get sick. And once in a while, it's also all right to have a sweet. But have you noticed all the people who spend their money on many kinds of foods which they don't even need and that are bad for their bodies? Have you seen how many children and parents eat so much more than they need and how unhealthy they become? Have you seen how people spend too much time thinking about food, buying it, cooking in complex ways, or going to restaurants? Some people are so busy with food, they forget to thank the One who gives it to them."

Layla piped up, "I guess it's the same with clothes! We don't need so many dresses and shoes, do we? I don't even wear a lot of my clothes. I am happy you give them to other children who do need them."

"Yes," said Haajar, "it's true, we all spend too much of our precious time just buying more and more clothes, more than we need. Most of us have way too many clothes! And then think of our homes! We need a home to protect us and cover us from weather, but some people spend their time and money just decorating and re-decorating, over and over, and perfecting their houses rather than their hearts! Making them more and more beautiful, but forgetting to make their hearts beautiful."

Layla pointed out, "Yes, Mommy! It must cost a lot to do that and there are poor people who need some of that money which is being used to just add extra things to houses."

"What a good and beautiful thought that is, Layla! We are spending a lot of our money on food, clothes, and things for the home that we don't really need, at the same time poorer people are in real need. We are busy all day long doing too much, more than we really need to, caring for these three simple needs. Imam al-Ghazali reminds us that learning and knowledge are greater than wealth and having so many things that we have to protect. What we *learn* guards and protects *us*."

"Yes, Mommy, I think I understand, but all of us can try to do better, can't we? If we don't waste our precious time just on eating and clothes, then we will have more time for Allah ﷻ and a better chance for going to the Heavenly Garden. We surely don't want to be so busy with eating and clothes that we forget why we were born and where we are going!"

"That is right, my dear daughter. We need to feed the heart as well as protect and give it shelter! Allah ﷻ promised *He* would give us what we need in this world. And now that we have all that straight, let's get you into your pajamas!"

Imam al-Ghazali

The Book of Knowledge For Children

"Mother, are the things we do, like sharing our toys, telling the truth, helping our mothers and fathers, not getting angry, and saying our prayers-are they like our shining good jewels inside our heart treasure chest?"

Chapter 10
Sharing the Treasure

Layla's sister, Zainab, who was eleven, waited for their mother to get Layla ready for bed. Layla still had to brush her teeth. Watching her, Zainab had a thought that she spoke out loud. "Mother, I have a body with two hands, two feet, and a head with a face. What does Imam al-Ghazali say is the best part of the body?"

"Great question, Zainab," said her mother. Haajar loved to talk about Imam al-Ghazali because she had loved his writings all her life, and her happiest times were when she was sharing her knowledge with her children. "Imam al-Ghazali says that the best part of the body is the heart, the *special, invisible* spiritual heart. Many people think that the brain is the most important part, and it is very important because we need the brain to think. Allah ﷻ wants us to be intelligent and thoughtful. But it is only deep in the spiritual heart that one can truly know God ﷻ, for the heart alone shines with His beauty and love. We are told it is this special heart, which once polished, can shine brightly. We have thoughts in our heads and brains, and we need to think. But thinking can only get you to know *about* Allah ﷻ. The heart helps you to know *Him*. So the heart is the *best* part of us. And the better we become, the closer we get to God ﷻ, and the more our hearts shine. Can you imagine your heart glowing with light? The heart inside of us is our very best treasure."

"Mother, are the things we do, like sharing our toys, telling the truth, helping our mothers and fathers, not getting angry, and saying our prayers—are they like our shining jewels inside our heart treasure chest?"

"Oh Zainab, exactly! And do you think you should keep these jewels of good deeds locked up in the storehouse of treasures?"

"No, Mother! We need to give these good deeds away to everybody we know—all the time! We must always be sharing the jewels inside our hearts! Then we will be happy all the time."

My girls are really understanding what is going on in this world!, Haajar thought to herself. She recalled that Imam al-Ghazali mentioned in his *Book of Knowledge* that the essence of the child, received from God ﷻ, gives children the ability from birth to *know* what is possible and what is not, and this essence directs them toward faith in God ﷻ. Children *naturally* cannot bear to hear lies or see injustice. For this reason, Haajar understood the importance of teaching her children the meanings and truths of their faith, which they would be able to recognize easily, especially while young.

Imam al-Ghazali

The Book of Knowledge For Children

"Yes, I can watch these ideas and thoughts and be like a guard at the castle gate. I will say "NO!" to them!! I can DO that."

Chapter 11
What Are Things You Must Learn

"Father, what are the most important things I should be learning from my family and my teachers?" Abdullah often asked his father Hamza questions while his mother was helping the girls to get ready for bed.

"Abdullah, that is a wonderful question! There are so many things to learn about in your lifetime. You are right to want to be sure you know what needs to be at the very top of your list! These would be what Allah ﷻ Himself has asked you to learn and find out about. As you get older, you will need to know how to offer the *salat* or daily prayer, how to fast in the month of Ramadan, how to give charity to the poor, and how to hopefully make the Hajj to Mecca. These are things you will learn as you grow up."

"But Father, what can I do *now*? What can children do now?"

"Oh, of course!" said his father, smiling. "I see what you are asking. Children can learn a lot of important things. They can learn how to be good and kind, and how to stay away from things that are ugly and wrong. There are wonderful things you can love doing now and there are other things you can watch out for, things that can harm us."

"Father, what kinds of things can *hurt* us?"

"Well, the Prophet ﷺ said our hearts are harmed if we are greedy."

"What does 'greedy' mean exactly? Wanting what someone

else has on top of what you already have?"

"Yes, but there's more to it than just that. A greedy person always wants more and more and is not happy with what he or she has. Even when a cake is being cut, that person wants the biggest piece, forgetting to be generous to others."

"But sometimes I really want the biggest piece of cake and also to have what belongs to my brother and sisters. I am going to watch myself and try to catch myself doing this. I don't want to be a greedy boy! Ever! And what else can *harm* us? What else do I need to watch out for?"

"Well, have you ever noticed that sometimes, some naughty ideas pop into your mind? Like maybe not doing what your mother asks you to do. Maybe you think about someone in your class whom you do not like and have the idea of doing something unkind to that child. Abdullah, if a bad idea comes into your thoughts, like wanting to show off, simply say 'No!' Can you think of a naughty thought that you caught yourself thinking and then you refused to do anything about?"

"Yes, I can watch these ideas and thoughts and be like a guard at a castle gate. I will say 'No!' to them! I can do that!" Abdullah nodded. "And if you ask me to get ready for bed, I won't pretend I didn't hear you calling to me."

"Ahh, I wondered about that," laughed his father. "I was wondering if you had lost your hearing!"

Abdullah blushed.

"And one more thing, the Prophet ﷺ told us that it also harms our hearts when we are conceited."

"What does that word mean?" asked Abdullah.

"Well, Abdullah, girls or boys who are conceited think just about themselves only and not others. They think that they are better than other boys and girls and get puffed up. They want all the attention! Have you ever been that way?"

Abdullah blushed again. "Oh, I think so—a little bit. Sometimes I only think about what I want and about me, Father. And I try to get your attention away from others. I want you to only think about me! But I can watch myself! I don't want to be a conceited boy."

Father Hamza explained, "For any bad that we do, we need to understand where it comes from and what harm it can do. Then we need to do the very opposite. Instead of being greedy, what can you decide to do instead?

Abdullah exclaimed, "Be generous! Share!"

"Exactly, son!" said Hamza. "Now get ready for bed. It's getting late."

As he stood up, Abdullah thought to himself, *This is going to be fun, like a game where I get to guard a castle gate and defend it!*

The Book of Knowledge For Children

"Where do the things we are supposed to learn come from?"

70

Chapter 12
Where Do the Wonderful Things We Can Learn Come From?

The next morning, after breakfast, Father Hamza drove little Bilal to school. On the way, Bilal, who was seven, asked his father, "Where do the things we are supposed to learn come from?"

"Well, son," Hamza replied, "that is a really important question! If somebody told you to do something every day of your life, like praying, how would you know for sure that this person was not just making up that duty? Or if you saw something in a book, how do you know that the person who wrote that book was a truthful and good person?"

Bilal said, "Sometimes I even tell stories and make up things and games. I tell my sister Layla to come into the pretend magic forest to meet a scary tiger king. But I just was making the game up myself, for fun. It's easy to make things up."

"Exactly! So where do we find out about the real things that we need to know or do? Well, God ﷻ sent the Angel Gabriel to our Prophet Muhammad ﷺ, telling us how to best live every day and then how to return to Him and enter Paradise at the end of our lives. All of these words from Allah ﷻ were written down and that is what the Holy Quran is!"

"Oh, now, I see why the Quran is so important to learn! I will listen better in my lessons," commented Bilal.

Hamza added, "And also we are so very blessed that we can know all about our Prophet Muhammad ﷺ, how he really looked, how he did things, what he actually said."

"Well, if we know how he did everything and the kind of person he was, then it would be easy to copy him and try to be like him!" Bilal exclaimed.

"Exactly, Bilal! How bright you are! That is why it is *easy* to be good and do the correct good thing, because we have the blessed Prophet ﷺ to copy! And do you know what 'copying' is called?"

Bilal said, "I think so, but maybe I forgot."

Hamza loved Bilal very much because he was a little boy who always told the truth. "It's called 'following the *sunna*.' The *sunna* is everything we know about that the Prophet ﷺ said, how he looked, and how he treated other people."

"But how do we know all that about him, if he lived so long ago? And how do we know that what we are told is true? Maybe somebody made it up like a story. How do we know about the *sunna* if he lived so long ago?"

"Excellent question. Well, you see our Prophet ﷺ had many excellent and very honest friends who carefully wrote down what he said and did. We know the names and about the pious lives of each of these people. This is what a *hadith* is. Have you heard that word? It comes from the Arabic verb *ha-da-tha*, which means to tell or relate. Can you imagine that we today can read these *hadiths* and thereby have the perfect life of the Prophet Muhammad ﷺ to follow and guide us to be beautiful in our hearts and life each day? Isn't it amazing how Allah ﷻ made the world, the trees, and the animals? Then He made us and sent the angel with His words to the Prophet Muhammad ﷺ so we wouldn't be confused about what we need to be doing in this world. God made *all* this for *us*!"

"Yes, I see, Father! If God ﷻ didn't send us rules, imagine how confusing everything could be! If there were no rules at school and no rules here at home, what would happen to us? Our life would be a mess!" Bilal exclaimed.

"Yes, son, God ﷻ lets us know *exactly* how to make Him happy with us and how to live happy, joyful lives."

Bilal said, "This is what *I* want to be like! I want to know what God ﷻ loves and make you and mother very happy! And everybody else, too!"

They had arrived at the school. Bilal jumped out and waved goodbye to his father. He saw his friends playing near the door and ran to join them.

The Book of Knowledge For Children

After dinner, the family sat around the campfire under the stars.

Chapter 13
More About the Two Worlds:
A Family Trip

One day Hamza and Haajar took their four children on a camping trip to a beautiful park near a mountain. Everyone helped to pack up the car with what they would need. Bilal and Abdullah helped their father fold and pack the tent that the family would sleep in at night. They made sure there were enough sleeping bags. Layla and Zainab made sandwiches for the road trip, and helped prepare the baskets of food needed for camping. Once their clothes and some kites and balls were packed as well, the family happily set out on their journey.

During the long drive, Zainab asked, "Is this trip we are on like the one Mommy told me about where we are traveling on a journey to the Garden in the Next World?"

Father Hamza replied, "Good for you, Zainab! Yes, we are driving to a beautiful park full of mountains and streams and birds. It's a small trip we are taking in *this* world, where we live right now. Later on, we will make the big journey to Paradise but the Next World will be more beautiful than we can ever imagine!"

Bilal asked, "What will we need to take on that trip? Will we need a tent, sleeping bags, and food to cook outside?"

Haajar joined in, "Don't you remember the story I read to you children about polishing our hearts? That's what we need to do for the journey to the most beautiful and perfect Heavenly Garden! That's *all* we need to do!"

Bilal replied, "I remember now, Mother! In order to make our hearts shine, we need to do all the things Allah ﷻ asks us to do! And these are written in the Quran which the angel brought from God ﷻ to our Prophet ﷺ!"

"Right!" exclaimed, Layla. "We must be very, very good. We need to help Mommy and Daddy and be very sweet to everybody and work hard to learn more and more!"

Father Hamza said, "*Al-hamdulilah!* I have such sweet and intelligent children! I am so glad you can understand about the two worlds. What fun we will have camping on this trip that we are on together in *this* world. And imagine how marvelous it will be for us, later on, to be forever and ever in the next most wonderful and perfect world together."

The children were looking out of the car windows, watching animals scurrying away from their car. They thought they saw some deer.

Soon the family arrived at the campsite. There was a small stream and everyone went wading in the water. Abdullah saw a golden fish, and Bilal caught a tiny frog. Layla went flower picking with Zainab, who also collected kindling for the fire that night. Abdullah went with Bilal before dinner to find big dry tree branches for the fire. After dinner, the entire family sat around the fire under the stars.

As he gazed up into the sky, Bilal asked his mother, "Could you tell us something from the Quran? Something the angel Gabriel told the Prophet ﷺ?"

"Well, let me see. I will tell you something *very* important. It might seem hard to understand, but then I will explain it and try to make it easy for you. In the Quran, God ﷻ tells us,

'Man does not receive other than that for which he strives.' (Q 53:39). That means we actually get exactly what we go after in this life, as well as the Next Life! Children, have you noticed that when you want something very, very much, you keep on trying to get it? You try different ways. Let's say you want us, your parents, to take you somewhere and to buy you something. You say, 'Oh Mother, please!,' you keep on asking us, don't you? You are *striving*, trying hard to get what you want. There are also many things you *don't* want, so for them you don't try or make any effort. Let's pretend you are playing a game and want to win and make the goal or hit the target. You try very hard, and finally you win! Whatever you try hard to get or achieve in school or games is what you actually get, or receive." Haajar smiled.

Father Hamza continued, "This is the same for your lives. If you work hard at becoming a good and lovely person in this life, in order to live forever in the Garden of the Next Life, then God ﷻ will reward you with that which you seek. But if you make *no* effort, no effort at all, what do you think will happen?"

"Then nothing good will happen," said Bilal.

"Precisely. What happens if you neglect your invisible, special heart and instead all you strive for in this life is stuff like money and clothes and popularity? Do you think any of this will make you happy? Will any of this connect you with your special, invisible heart and with God ﷻ, Who is the source of all happiness? No, of course not. These things won't keep you happy, and then you'll want more and more things to make you happy, but then you'll find that you are still not really happy."

Mother added, "Your life will *look like* what you are trying to get. If you decide all you want is to make money and be rich on the outside of your being, your whole life will look like that! Everyone will notice that your life is full of *stuff*, and you will always worry about getting still more *stuff*. You will be suffering and sad because you want more and more, and are not happy with what Allah ﷻ gave to you.

"There is a *hadith* that says, 'If the child of Adam had two valleys full of gold, he wouldn't be satisfied until he has a third!' For example, you may be happy with your games or toy airplane but when you see what your friend has, you then are not happy until you have that as well. It never seems to end!"

Zainab chimed in, "It is true. I only wanted a bicycle just like my friend Mona has. And now I want a basket for the bike."

Hamza added, "People live their lives seeking happiness in all the wrong places! Then, as they die, they realize the mistake, and no longer want more *things* because at last they see that all stuff is like dust; it is finally meaningless. Some never connect with their invisible, special hearts, the one and only thing that can fill them with light and beauty, instead of dust. So this *hadith* is telling us that most people can never be satisfied and just keep wanting more and more."

The children listened and thought about how much their toys and games meant to them. Their father explained further. "But you, children, on the other hand can, in fact, be free of all that worry and suffering and endlessly wanting more and more things. How? You can instead try to get *real* knowledge, the kind that shows you how to make your heart shine and be full of happiness and joy! You are blessed if your goal is simply *trying* to be pure, lovely people, the kind of people you notice that you really like."

The children nodded in agreement. There were a lot of peaceful, wise people whom they truly admired.

Mother Haajar concluded, "So, you see, you can make your efforts to become a beautiful person inside your heart and on the outside, too, by the way you live your life each day."

"And then that's what you will get in this life if you go after a beautiful way of *being*," Hamza added. "And no one can ever take all the good things you do and the good person you are from you. What you get can never be lost or broken like a toy. It's yours forever in this world and the Next. And because your heart is filled with light, you will go to Paradise where all your dreams come true!"

Haajar said, "As Imam al-Ghazali reminds us, we are told in Islam that whoever makes his pilgrimage or journey through this life to get things and just have a good time entertaining himself, well, that's all he will wind up with and that's what his life will be made up of! But whoever makes his or her trip or journey through this life trying to please God ﷻ and to be a beautiful and loving being—well, that's what your life will look like!! And that's what you will get to keep forever!"

"Mommy and Daddy, thank you so much for explaining to us about the two ways we can choose to live!" Layla burst out. "I want to learn more and more ways to have a shining heart, and how to have what I will need so I can go to the Garden of Paradise with you and everybody I love."

Bilal added, "Now I understand what's happening! You know, I have seen the two kinds of people you talked about, Mother. I can see what their faces look like. We see our grandmother who always thinks of God ﷻ and tells us wonderful stories. Her day is filled with helping others and prayers. Look at her face! It's shining! She's so beautiful and peaceful. We love her!"

Zainab added, "Her heart is shining! I can see she is all lit up with light!"

Father added, "Yes, children, full of light. In Arabic, the word for light is *nur*. And when we see dear, precious people like this, we say that he or she is *munawwar* or full of light. We can see this!"

Layla wondered whether or not they should tell their parents about wise Haj Abdullah. He was one of those people their parents seemed to be talking about. He didn't seem to have *anything,* but he was noble and dignified. When the children spoke, he listened carefully to each word and was completely present for them. Most adults didn't pay attention to children.

Abdullah added, "And it is sad to see faces that are dark. I want to have a shining face!"

Zainab exclaimed, "Oh, yes! Let's learn all the ways how to shine!"

"Yes, let's," said Haajar. "But for now we all need to get a good night's sleep. Tomorrow we will go hiking and swimming. In the evening, around the fire, we can continue learning about the lessons al-Ghazali brought to us to help us live a shining life."

"But Mommy . . ." Layla began.

"Now it is time for you to lay your little head down and get a good night's rest. Look up at all the stars in the sky! I'll have a question ready for you the moment I wake up," promised Haajar.

Imam al-Ghazali

You can't go up to the next step until you have learned everything there is to learn on the step where you are! The Prophet ﷺ said that whoever travels a path of knowledge, God will cause him to journey upon a path that leads to the Garden of Paradise.

Chapter 14
Two Kinds of Things You Can Learn—
Knowledge That Makes Your Heart Shine

What a beautiful night the family spent camping. Snug in their sleeping bags, it was hard for anyone to really sleep as they gazed at the moon and stars shining so brightly. What fun they had cooking breakfast over the fire. The children ran off to play. Mother packed a picnic that the family took with them on their hike to the mountain.

By noon, the family reached a clear, blue babbling brook. The children thought it would be fun to dangle their feet over the edge of the bank as everyone ate a delicious sandwich. They all gazed up towards the top of the majestic mountain.

Mother Haajar asked Zainab, "Tell us one thing that you *know* is true!"

Zainab thought for a moment and said, "Well, I know that the grass is green and mountains are tall, and I know that there are daytimes and nights. And I know what is right and wrong."

Bilal said, "And what we know about is called *knowledge*! But are there different kinds of knowledge?"

Father Hamza replied, "There are lots of things we need to know about for our everyday life, like how to drive a car and cook food. Zainab said we know grass is green! But she also said we know what is right from what is wrong."

"So besides knowing about things, and how to do things, there are also *two* kinds of very special Real Knowledge. One kind of Real Knowing is what helps us to become good people and is what we need in order to go to the *next* very special world. As you know, that is why Allah ﷻ sent us the Quran and our Prophet Muhammad ﷺ so we can know what is right and what is wrong, and then know how to do what is right and how to polish our hearts so they will shine and sparkle—just the way light shines off polished mirrors!"

Layla asked, "What is the *other* Real Knowing you talked about, Father? You said there are two kinds of knowing! The first is knowing what is right and wrong to do."

"Well, Layla the second kind of knowledge is most important. This teaches us exact ways to make our hearts shining and full of light. Learning this is very precious, like a special secret! You can see what happens to people who do this, who have this special secret. It shines in the faces of those who have it and lights up what they do and who they are."

"You can see it on the faces of beautiful people whose hearts are really pure. They cleaned their hearts of every little thing that was not so nice. And then, when they had worked hard and their hearts were clean, this light just shines from inside them. And God ﷻ teaches these pure people many special things, like why He made us and why He made this world!"

"Daddy, can you tell me more?" begged Layla. "Can I know those special secrets, too?"

"Well, let me explain to you children. It's like climbing up steps. Learning is like a staircase or ladder. Imagine you are standing at the bottom of a ladder that goes very high up into the sky. Would you try to rush up that ladder or stairs as fast as you could?"

"Rush up a really high ladder?" Abdullah asked. "No way! I might trip and fall."

"So how would you climb it?" Father continued.

"We'd go slowly, step by step, and make sure that our feet didn't slip," chimed in Zainab.

"Exactly!" said Father. "And that's the way it is with learning special knowledge. You can't go to the next step until you learn all you can on the step you're on."

"Oh, I see," said Abdullah, "like before I could read, I needed to learn letters!"

"Precisely!" Mother Haajar continued, "And when we reach the very top of these stairs, we are like birds in the sky, and we will see the world below as one whole and glorious creation of God ﷻ. Then we will understand with a sure knowledge that there is no God ﷻ but Him. At this moment, we become our special invisible hearts, and we see things as they truly are! The place we are climbing toward is so high we can't even see where it is now. We can't even see what's on top of the mountain from here, can we? The kind of learning we need, to climb all the way up, is called *mystical.* It's a mystery to us now but as we finally climb up these steps of learning during our lives, we will understand everything very clearly. We will no longer have doubts."

Hamza added, "We will be able to see clearly and feel very close to God ﷻ. We will know not just with our minds and senses, but in our hearts."

As they left the mountain, Zainab and Bilal noticed some secret hidden steps going up toward some bright light. As they ran up the steps to see what was there, their parents called them back.

Haajar and Hamza and the children packed up the tent and everything they had brought from the city and headed back home. In the car on the way back, they shared songs and rhymes that Haajar had taught them when they were younger. The children very much enjoyed learning from their parents and each other, but they were very excited to get back to the secret place in the neighborhood's forgotten secret garden to hear what Haj Abdullah had to say next.

Imam al-Ghazali

The Book of Knowledge For Children

Imagine you have two wolves living inside your head: a good one that tells you to do good things and a bad one that suggests you do naughty things. Which do you feed?

Chapter 15
The Story of the Two Wolves

The children had not gathered in the secret meeting place for a few days and were eager to get back to their friends and the stories of Haj Abdullah.

"Welcome back!" cried Qasim.

"We're glad to be back," said Zainab and Abdullah in unison. Then they nudged each other for the fun of saying the same thing at the same time.

"Stop that, you two," said Layla.

"Yes, the sooner you settle down, the sooner we can hear that story Haj Abdullah promised us when we returned from camping."

"A tale from the Cherokee Indians, right?"

"Yes," said the elder, "good memory. It's a story they tell their children. Shall we begin?"

Everyone settled in closely. They were eager to listen.

"Imagine, dear children, that you have two pretend wolves living inside your head. There is a beautiful, good wolf that tells you to do good things and a mean, bad one that suggests you do naughty things. These two wolves are always fighting. Which one will win? The one you feed. So you see, it's better to starve the bad wolf by not listening to it at all. Do not listen to it when it tells you to say something bad about someone else. Do not listen to it when it tells you to whine or be in a bad mood. If you do what it tells you, it's like you are feeding it and you are only making it stronger. Tell the bad, mean wolf to run away deep into the forest and to never come back. The more you tell that bad wolf it is not welcome, the weaker and weaker it will grow, and one day it will just disappear and wither away. It will never feel it is welcome in your precious life. Pay attention instead to the beautiful, good wolf who reminds you to listen to your parents and to speak to others only with kind words. That kind wolf is the one you want to get stronger.

"But we know it is not easy. Every day we must ask ourselves many times which wolf will we feed. And I mean grown-ups, too, children, both young and old, we are all facing the same struggles, the same two pretend wolves within ourselves. So let's help each other and only listen to our good wolves. Together, with the help of God ﷻ, we can do this."

Haj Abdullah folded his hands together on his lap and sat in silence.

Qasim chimed in, "Right! Don't give that wicked wolf the joy of your following his bad ideas!"

Amina said quietly, "Instead you are feeding the good wolf every single time you do the right thing."

"Amina and Yusuf," said Haj Abdullah solemnly, "you are learning how to get closer to Allah ﷻ. Stories like this remind us to watch our 'lower' selves and correct them. Later you will learn about your three selves."

The children could hardly wait! What *three* selves? So many of their questions were being answered by both their parents and their noble guide. As the sun began to set, rays of light fell upon the smiling, tranquil face of Haj Abdullah.

Imam al-Ghazali

The Book of Knowledge For Children

But you can see what happens when you are nice to someone and they become happy! You can see a smile on someone's face and know that you make them happy. But happiness is invisible.

Chapter 16
Important Things You Cannot See

The next afternoon following school, the children gathered at the secret place. They had been thinking about the story of the pretend wolves.

"But how do we know what is real and right if we cannot see it or touch it?" asked Maryam.

"Yes, like we understand that the story of the wolves is not real, but the story tells us about something that *is* true, that we understand in our hearts," added Yusuf.

Haj Abdullah explained, "There are so many things you can see and touch. You can see the trees outside. You can touch your toys, correct? But even so, a storm can tear down a tree or a toy can fall to pieces! Some things, however, can never be broken! Do you know what lasts forever and can never, ever be lost or broken?"

The children were all silent, thinking about what Haj Abdullah asked.

He continued, "Think about what you cannot see that can never be taken away or broken. For example, you can't see love or kindness. But you can see what happens when you are nice to someone and they become happy. You can see a smile on someone's face and know that you make them happy. But happiness is invisible. There are so many things that you can't see or touch that make you very happy and that can never be taken from you. If you tell the truth or do the right thing, those are invisible good deeds that you get to keep, always!

Your parents love you! You can't see love, but you can see all the good it does, can't you? And how it feels inside you. You can't see the feeling of anger itself, but you can notice all the bad things that come from it. What is something you can see that you like? What is something you can't see with your eyes but that you like very much?"

Maryam said softly, "I like my friends at school. I can see them with my eyes. But what *feels* best is when we include someone who might be left out."

"And I like to help Madame Dina when she comes home from the market with too many bags," said Qasim.

"Both of you describe something that is good. You, Amina, describe kindness and consideration, which you cannot see but you feel is good and right. Qasim, you tell about helpfulness, which you also cannot see but which is good and right. These are both good doings that can never be taken away from you. They are *part* of you. When you have these, they are as real as a toy or a plate of food. But even better!" commented the elder.

The sun had slipped below the horizon and it was time for the children to go back to their families. They all bid Haj Abdullah a good evening and he, in turn, nodded with respect, and smiled at each child. He made each one feel special. He seemed to be speaking directly to their *real* hearts.

Imam al-Ghazali

The Book of Knowledge For Children

"What we learn is like LIGHT and we want to be at our very best when we receive Allah's ﷻ Light," Layla added. "So when I have my lesson, I want to be clean and tidy. I will sit up straight. Watch me. I can do it all the time, too! When I do that, it always feels so good!" But we are learning all the time, every single minute, aren't we?"

Chapter 17
More Ways to Make Your Heart Shine! and The Four Imams

Bilal woke up thinking about his invisible, spiritual heart. He asked his father Hamza, "Could you tell me some ways I can be polishing my heart every day?"

"Son, what an important question! Imam al-Ghazali shares with us those secrets that teach us how to fill our hearts with light. These ways came from people who lived before him and were passed down like an unbroken chain from generation to generation, all the way down to us today. One of those original teachers of the heart, of true learning, was a man named Imam Shafi'i. Imam Shafi'i was one of four teachers in ancient, earlier times who are considered some of the best teachers of the heart, just like al-Ghazali was in his time. Imam Shafi'i wrote down these many wonderful teachings, and he organized them, in a way that is easy to understand. He helped so many people, but he never wanted anyone to thank him. All he wanted was God's ﷻ reward not theirs. He did his good deeds quietly and secretly, just because it was the correct thing to do, and this brought his secret, invisible heart great happiness."

Bilal said, "That was because Allah ﷻ knows everything, and so Allah ﷻ knew that the reason he didn't tell people all the good he did was because he did it only for God ﷻ and not for people. I can understand that both thinking well of myself and showing off harms my heart."

"Exactly! So Bilal, tell me something you can do like Imam Shafi'i did to help make your heart shine."

"Well, Father, I could pick up my toys after I play with them, without being asked, in order to *secretly* help mother. Will doing that good thing be waiting for me in the Garden of Paradise when we go there?"

"It certainly will! And I am sure you can think of more ideas like that many times a day. I am so proud of you when you think of ways to be at your best."

Layla piped up, "And Mother told me that Imam Shafi'i did a very nice thing, the kind that also brightens the heart."

"What is that, Layla? Is it something you can do, too?"

"Actually yes, Daddy. When Imam Shafi'i was discussing something with anyone, he wanted his friend to be right, not wrong. He wanted the best for his friend, that his friend should be right and that *only* truth should win out. So what I can do, and it's not that hard, is when Bilal and I don't agree, I can really want very, very much for him to be the one who's right. It's all right and even easy, for me to be wrong about something. It doesn't matter, does it? What is important is not that a person is right but that what is true should be said."

"How true! What matters is that you really want the very best for others—that they tell the correct answer. It doesn't always have to be you!" Haajar said.

"Mommy, I do want the very best for others, and I will try to always remember to copy what Imam Shafi'i did. But it's not easy."

Abdullah then asked, "But Father, you said there were four great men, great teachers of the heart who taught the true learning, what we need to know and what we need to do in order to strengthen our special, invisible hearts. Who were the other teachers? I want to learn from them, too! Tell me something about each one of them that I can learn from."

Hamza replied, "Another great teacher was a man named Imam Malik. In fact, he was Imam al-Shafi'i's teacher. Imam Malik lived in Medina, the city where the Prophet ﷺ lived and is buried. People appreciated and loved him and were so grateful to Imam Malik for all that he did, that people brought him many gifts. But when they left, he gave all the lovely gifts away to people who were in need."

Abdullah commented, "What a good thing to do! I have more than I need, and I could share what I have, too. Making people happy is more important than having things."

Zainab exclaimed, "What else can you tell us about Imam Malik, Daddy?"

"For one thing, when he was getting ready to teach, he had such love and respect for the lessons and knowledge, that he did *wudu'*, to be pure and clean, then combed his hair neatly, made sure his clothes were tidy and clean, and then he sat up very straight with dignity. Someone asked him why he did all this. He explained that what we learn is like light, and we want to be at our very best when we receive God's ﷻ light."

Layla added, "So when I have my lesson, I want to be clean and tidy. I will sit up straight. Watch me! I think I can do it most of the time, too. When I do that, it always feels so good!"

"We are learning all the time, every single minute, aren't we?" Haajar said.

And Father Hamza added, "When Imam Malik was asked lots of questions, he wasn't shy about answering most of them by simply saying truthfully 'I don't know.' Imam al-Ghazali mentions he was like a star piercing through the darkness. By always telling the truth, your mind will remain clear."

Haajar concluded, "I am very glad you children have heard about Imam Shafi'i and Imam Malik. Besides them there were two other great Imams named Imam Abu Hanifa and Imam Ahmad ibn Hanbal. As you grow up you will learn more about their beautiful lives, how they lived with only what they really needed, how they prayed even late during the night when others were all sleeping, and how they gave their lives to help others. Once, Abu Hanifa overheard someone praising something he did. But he felt ashamed that this was not something he did *all* the time. He was embarrassed that God ﷻ would know this. From then on, he did what he was praised for."

Hamza added, "What made them so special and so noble? The answer is that they learned and came to know in their deepest hearts a higher kind of special learning called *divine* learning! That special knowledge has been understood to be like a light which appears in a heart that is pure, and leads on to understanding deeper and higher meanings and nearness to Allah ﷻ."

"Father, how can we learn about that very high and special learning and knowing? How do we climb these steps one by one to this special place of understanding and knowing about how to do truly good deeds?" asked Abdullah.

Hamza explained, "That is exactly what these books that Imam al-Ghazali wrote are all about! Bless him! He is giving you all special, special learning. Imagine being simply given the best thing you will ever need in the whole world!"

"Having Imam al-Ghazali as our teacher makes us so lucky!" exclaimed Zainab.

"Better than lucky," said Haajar, "blessed."

Imam al-Ghazali

The Book of Knowledge For Children

The ant thought the pen was writing the words by itself!

Chapter 18
The Ant and the Pen

Haj Abdullah had arrived at the secret meeting place before the children again. He always looked serene and peaceful, as if he had a light shining from within.

"He looks luminous," whispered Yusuf. "I learned that word in school today. It means glowing. Like he has a little sun inside that shines through him."

Haj Abdullah cleared his throat. "Let me tell you Imam al-Ghazali's marvelous story about an ant. Once upon a time, an ant was walking across a piece of paper and was looking at the words being written upon its surface, all the black lines made of ink. The ant thought to herself, *What a great and clever pen! It writes these nice words that have meanings on this page!*" Haj Abdullah paused. "But children, is it really the pen that's writing all by itself?"

"No!" they answered together.

"It's a person who has the pen in her hand, and her hand is at the end of her arm," said Amina.

"Exactly right," Haj Abdullah answered. "So why does that little ant think it's the pen writing on its own?"

"Because she's too little," explained Ahmad, "to see the hand and the arm and the person."

"Correct again," agreed the smiling elder. "But let me ask you something else. Who made that person with a hand and an arm and a brain? Who helps her even to be able to write?"

"It's God ﷻ," said Yusuf, "Who made everything and everyone. The ant was just so little that she could only see the pen."

"True!," said Haj Abdullah, "and the ant couldn't see God ﷻ."

Abdullah jumped in. "But what does this story mean? Why did Imam al-Ghazali write a story about an ant?"

"Excellent question, Abdullah! So let's try to see the hidden, secret message sent to us in this story. Pretend you all are ants. Then I, the grandfather ant, tell you that we are not going on a trip we had planned to the zoo. What do you young ants say?"

Layla cried out, "We would whine and say 'But you promised us! We were looking forward to the zoo today! Why, oh why, can't we go? We want to go!'"

Haj Abdullah said, "So the grandfather ant explains that ant relatives and family are coming to visit, and that is why the zoo trip has been cancelled. But the children ants are sad and mope about with sad faces. The next day, the ant family hears on the radio that a big dangerous lion got out of the cage at the zoo exactly at the very time when the ant family would have been there!"

"Oh my!" said Maryam. "A lion. With big teeth and claws!"

Haj Abdullah explained, "So you see children, just like the ant who couldn't see the person holding the pen, or Allah ﷻ who made that person, the ant-children who didn't get to go to the zoo, couldn't see, or know, that a dangerous lion would be breaking out of his cage! We can't always see that it is Allah ﷻ who makes some things happen and other things not happen."

Bilal cried out, "But God ﷻ knew about the lion because He

knows everything even before it happens!"

"And," offered Zainab, "because God ﷻ loves the baby ants, he fixed it so they couldn't go to the zoo where the lion might have eaten them! So God ﷻ sent the ant relatives and cousins to visit in order to save the baby ants!"

Bilal exclaimed, "Yes! Sometimes we're like the ants! We think we didn't go to the zoo because our cousins came, but *really* it was because God ﷻ wanted to protect us from getting hurt, so He sent our cousins just at that moment!"

The wise elder explained, "Children, the lesson from the ant story is one of the most important you will ever learn. When things happen, or don't happen, it is because Allah ﷻ is trying to take care of you!"

Qasim added, "So we are small and our brains are not able to know all that is happening in God's ﷻ careful, loving plan. So we *trust* Him! He made us, and only He can know everything that is going on all over the whole world, all the time!"

Maryam went on, "Of course, we are disappointed at times if things don't work out for us the way we thought they would, but if we remember this story we will remember to trust what happens in our lives and try our best to see with our hearts what lessons can be learned. Life is about learning and becoming wiser."

Ahmad concluded with excitement, "Sometimes we can't go to the zoo or do some other fun thing that we looked forward to. But now we know that in our hearts, deep inside, we know to trust what Allah ﷻ is doing and what things He makes happen in our lives."

"All right," said Bilal, "I will just have to learn how to be happy no matter what! Because it is what God ﷻ is doing and He always gives us what we need most, even if it looks hard to get through!"

"The baby ants were sad because they didn't know God ﷻ was saving them from the lion! But we are people, not ants!" Layla insisted.

"Yes, right, Layla! And we have been given Imam al-Ghazali who is telling us how to see the world with intelligent thoughtful hearts and about how life and the world really work. We are human beings, and we can learn and know."

Haj Abdullah raised his arms in a sweeping gesture, like a magnificent eagle. "Aren't we so greatly blessed, all of us?"

Imam al-Ghazali

The Book of Knowledge For Children

The wise grandfather said, "Maybe good, maybe bad."

Chapter 19
A Little Boy Loses His Father's Horse

"Haj Abdullah, would you again please tell us the story of the little boy who lost his father's horse?"

"Ah, the tale from Central Asia?" Haj Abdullah said. "What do you like so much about this story, Ahmad?"

"I like it because it shows me why I should be happy with what I have and not want what others have or have been given by Allah ﷻ!"

"Wishing very much that you had what someone else was given by God ﷻ is a kind of envy," explained the elder. "We should always say *al-hamdulilah* for everything we have, all the time, because God ﷻ knows exactly what each of us needs to be good and beautiful on the inside. The Quran tells us that sometimes we want something very much and it turns out to be bad for us! And sometimes, something happens to us and we are sad, but it is really good for us!"

"Like the little ants!" Maryam exclaimed. "Please tell us that story again."

"As you wish," said the elder. "Once upon a time, there was a dear little boy named Omar. His family was very poor, but they did own a horse of which they were exceedingly proud. One day, Omar was out in the countryside, beyond the village, and the family's beautiful white horse ran off. When the news of this loss reached the people of the town, they ran to Omar's father who was considered to be a very wise elder. They exclaimed, 'Oh, father of Omar! We are so sad for your family! All you owned was the beautiful mare!'

"Abu Omar simply responded, without being upset, 'Maybe good, maybe bad.'

"The following morning, Omar went out into the valleys amidst the mountains in search of the lost horse. Lo and behold! He came across an entire herd of horses and was able to lead them back to the town where he safely enclosed the many horses inside a fenced corral. The town's folk ran to Omar's father, crying out with joy. 'Oh, Sir, you are so fortunate! Now you are rich because you have an entire herd of fine horses!'

"But the calm, wise elder merely remarked, 'Maybe good. Maybe bad.'

"Omar decided to pick out one of these horses to be his very own. He went into the corral to choose the one he most fancied. Suddenly, all of the horses became nervous and moved about frantically. Omar got badly stepped on and his leg was broken in many places. It was so bad that he wouldn't ever be able to walk again very well or play sports with the other boys. The villagers ran to his father wailing, 'Abu Omar! Your only son is now crippled! This is terrible news for your family.'

"The wise father responded, neither with sadness nor happiness, 'Maybe good, maybe bad.'

"At this time there was a war raging in that country. The king sent out his army to collect soldiers and young men to fight in the war. Most all of these young men, sadly, would never return home to their mothers and fathers. The morning after Omar's accident, the army reached his village. They went from house to house, taking all the young men and boys away to fight where they would probably be killed. Then they came to

Abu Omar's house. The sergeant knocked loudly on the door and when Omar's father opened it, he shouted rudely, 'We heard you have a son. Bring him out. We need him for the army!' Just then Omar came into the room. He was limping and walking with a stick.

"'That's your son?' shouted the sergeant.

"'Yes sir, that's my only boy.'

"'We can't use him!' the sergeant said rudely. 'We only need men and boys who can run fast.' And off he stormed angrily. When the news that Omar was not taken by the army reached the people of the village, they finally realized how wise Abu Omar was whenever he said, 'Maybe it's good, maybe it's bad.'

"So you see, his wise father had been right all along. When the villagers had come to him and said that the lost horse and the broken leg of his son Omar were very bad for the family, Omar's father left the matter up to God ﷻ, Who knew what would be happening. God ﷻ loved Omar, so He protected him from one day going off to fight in a terrible war. Instead, God ﷻ gave him two small trials, losing the family horse and having his leg very badly hurt. What the villagers thought was sad and bad news for Omar's family was, in fact, good!

"So, children, just say, 'Praise God ﷻ, *al-hamdulilah*,' no matter what happens, because you can't tell what God ﷻ has planned, can you? Something you don't like may happen but don't be sure it's good or bad! Allah ﷻ has your best in His plans for you, so just *watch* the ups and downs, like a see-saw, and thank Him for it all, the ups and the downs included."

The children all started chattering at once.

Haj Abdullah waited for them to quiet down. Then he continued,

"We have been talking about your Real Hearts. Would you like another story similar to that of the ant and the lost horse?"

"Oh, yes!" everyone cried out. "We love stories."

"Once there was a merchant who lived near the sea in Spain. He was waiting for his shipload of goods to arrive, goods that he would then sell. He was told, 'Oh, sir! We have heard the ship with your goods has sunk.'

"The merchant looked down at his heart and calmly said, "Praise God ﷻ *al-hamdulilah*.' A few weeks later the same young man ran to the merchant and this time joyfully announced, 'Oh, merchant! Your boat did *not* sink after all. All of your goods are being unloaded now on the dock.'

"The merchant simply stated, '*al-hamdulilah*' as he gazed again toward his heart.

"The young man asked, 'Why, when I brought you both good and bad news, did you look down at your heart?'

"The merchant replied, 'At both times, I wanted to be *sure* my heart didn't move but stayed still, resting in peace, trusting Allah ﷻ.'"

Haj Abdullah concluded, "So, my dear children, how have these stories helped you?"

Qasim replied, "What we understand from them is that we don't have to worry because God ﷻ is taking care of our lives perfectly." "Yes," added Amina. "Our hearts need to stay calm and peaceful. We must remember to simply love what Allah ﷻ is giving us."

Imam al-Ghazali

The Book of Knowledge For Children

Layla said, "I can hardly wait to sit near angels and remember God ﷻ! What could be better than that?!

Chapter 20
The Little Gardens Inside the Garden

Back home that night, Bilal heard his grandparents talking with some of their friends. He always loved to listen to what grown-ups liked to speak about. His grandmother, Aisha, said that she read in Imam al-Ghazali's *Book of Knowledge* that the Garden of Paradise of the Next World has smaller gardens here on this earth.

Grandfather explained, "When groups of people sit and learn together in circles and remember God ﷻ, they are actually sitting in these *little gardens*."

Then Bilal heard Uncle Mahmud say something very, very exciting. He said, "Imam al-Ghazali mentioned that the Prophet ﷺ said God ﷻ has angels wayfaring through the sky, other than the angels that watch humankind. When they see us gathering for remembrance of God ﷻ, they call one another saying, 'Hasten to your heart's desire.' Then they surround this group and lower their wings over them and listen to what they are saying."

Bilal was thrilled. He told Layla, "Next time our grandparents and their friends gather to remember God ﷻ, let's join them so that we, too, can sit with the angels who come!"

Layla said, "I can hardly wait, Bilal, to sit near *angels* and remember God ﷻ! What could be better than that?!"

Just then Grandmother Aisha caught them peeking into the room. "What wonderful grandchildren you are! Let me tell you all one more amazing thing that Imam al-Ghazali has told us. If you join just one gathering of remembering God ﷻ, in which useful knowledge is taught, it makes up for seventy times when you joined with other people or your friends, and were just playing around, not doing anything truly great with your precious time! Imagine that."

She spread her arms wide to summon the children to her side. They gathered beside her to hear more about Imam al-Ghazali, Grandmother Aisha's favorite subject.

Imam al-Ghazali

The Book of Knowledge For Children

Here is my heart. I will color in dots which are the things I need to wipe away so my heart can shine without dust or dirt!

Chapter 21
How Can You Watch Your Very Own Hearts?

"Grandmother," Zainab asked, "you keep telling us that we need to keep our hearts really pure and make them shining. How do we do that?"

She answered, "Well, that is why we are reading the books of Imam al-Ghazali together. He is giving us a map to follow in order to become our *true* selves. He is telling us how to make our hearts filled with light because it is the most important thing we can do—more than anything else."

Zainab drew a golden heart on a piece of paper. She explained, "Here is my heart. I will now draw dots on it which are things I need to wipe from my heart so it can shine without dust or dirt!"

"Zainab, what a wonderful idea! That helps you to easily see the problems you are working to clear away! Everyone should draw hearts like that! Tell me about the specks of dust you have drawn. What do they mean to you?"

"Oh, well, this big red dot is for when I don't help Mother. Then that one is because I don't like to share my things. And the yellow one is for my showing off and having to be right all the time. So I will watch these dots. I will watch these problems inside my mind and heart. I want to make them smaller and smaller until they go away and vanish. I want them to go away and disappear. I will add more dots on this drawing as I notice other bad things in me, and I will label them. These bad things are like nasty weeds trying to stop my good deeds from growing. But I won't let them do that!"

Layla said, "Look! I am drawing my heart, too! This big blue dot is because sometimes I don't tell the truth. And the big red dot is for when I cry to get what I want!"

"Oh, dear grandchildren. You are so bright and good. This idea of keeping a dot list will help you polish your special hearts and make it easy for you to polish off all the dust. New kinds of dust will come, as we are always tested in life. But you will be ready, watching and waiting, prepared to stop the dots of dust and dirt, the things you don't admire in yourselves. Yes, it's just like pulling up choking weeds that are sprouting in the garden of your heart."

Zainab exclaimed, "This is going to be fun! And is it true that if our hearts are all clean that we will go to the most beautiful Garden, the Garden of Heaven and Paradise in the Next World?"

Grandmother Aisha nodded. "Exactly! Let's watch and clean our hearts together every day. What a wonderful and even enjoyable effort this is, that we *get* to do! And just to make sure we cover all the bases, here is a list of ten bad things for the heart that al-Ghazali warns about, that I want you to watch out for." Grandmother wrote them down on a piece of paper where all the children could see them:

1. Envy
2. Lying
3. Pride
4. Being a Know-It-All
5. Wasting Our Time
6. Back-Biting
7. Bragging
8. Hypocrisy
9. Prying and Spying
10. Arguing

"But how will Imam al-Ghazali help us avoid these ten harmful things?" asked Abdullah.

"Let's go through them," said Grandmother. "We may not have time to get to all of them, but for these important subjects, we have all the time in the world tonight to try."

The Book of Knowledge For Children

That family has beautiful, shining faces and hearts. They have accepted the hardships, with trust, that God ﷻ has chosen to help them grow better

Chapter 22
Envy

Grandmother Aisha patted Layla's and Bilal's heads. "This question is for the little ones. Tell me about envy."

Layla answered, "Envy is bad! Because to envy is to want what somebody else has! And that is a very silly thing to do because God ﷻ has a very special plan for each one of us. And besides, envy is like a fire inside of someone and is very painful."

Grandmother confirmed, "The Imam reminds us that in just the same way fire eats up wood, envy eats up our good deeds. Indeed, dreadful!"

"Layla is right!" said Bilal. "There is a boy in my class at school named Ali who is in a wheelchair and will never be able to play or run like me. But you know what I noticed about Ali and his mother and father?"

"What, Bilal?" asked Grandmother Aisha. "What did you notice?"

"Well, I can see that they received different, but still very good and important, gifts from God ﷻ. They all have beautiful, pure faces and you can tell that all of their hearts are really shining. They have accepted the difficulty and hardship of Ali's trial for the family with trust and good hearts. They are so nice to everyone, and we all love being with them! I remember you told us that the best thing we can ever get in our lives is a pure heart full of light. And that a pure and shining heart is all we can take with us to the Garden of Paradise when we get to return to God ﷻ! But look at Ali and his family. Because they have this special hardship, they have been given a special reward. They have gotten shining hearts! That family is not wishing for the blessings that I have, envying me, because they are grateful to God ﷻ for their own *special* blessings. They say *al-hamdulilah* in thanks."

"See," said Grandmother, "you must never wish for or envy what blessings others have because then you cannot pay attention to Allah's ﷻ wonderful plan for you!"

Imam al-Ghazali

The Book of Knowledge For Children

Today I was not lazy!

Chapter 23
Having Pride and Being Spiteful

Grandmother Aisha then asked, "What are some other dangers that can cover our special, invisible hearts with dust and how can we prevent this?"

The children all jumped in.

"Being spiteful!"

"Being a back-biter!"

"Bragging!"

Grandmother held up her hand. "Yes, these are all dangers, but you are moving too fast. You have just learned what the word *envy* means: wanting what *others* have instead of being *very* happy with the particular blessings that God ﷻ chose for you! Our Prophet ﷺ told us that envy burns up good deeds and good things you have done. So if you feel it coming inside of you, look at it and what do you say?"

Zainab offered, "I say, 'No, envy, no! I love what God ﷻ chose to give me and chose to give my friends because He knows best what we really need to enter the Garden and come back to Him'!"

Grandmother smiled. "Now we are ready for the next big danger to your shining hearts.

Another harmful thing to watch out for is called pride."

Abdullah asked, "What does 'pride' mean, Grandmother? Please explain."

"A proud person is someone who thinks that he or she is better than other people and is puffed up with this pride and arrogance. Do you know any children like that? You don't like them very much, do you?"

Zainab exclaimed, "No, I don't! I don't like a girl in my class because she pretends to be better than the rest of us! She thinks she deserves to have the best seat on the first row all the time!"

"You should feel sorry for her, Zainab," said Grandmother. "The Prophet Muhammad ﷺ told us that Allah ﷻ will find ways to uplift the people who are humble, not pushing themselves up above others. God ﷻ will lift those people up, and honor them."

"I can see what you are saying! The man who sells us vegetables is very quiet and peaceful. We like to be with him," Abdullah added.

"Yes," said Grandmother, "and also there are women and men who are presidents of businesses, and also there are teachers who may have a lot, but also don't show off. They have humility, not pride!"

"And there is more," added Grandfather Muhammad, not wanting this precious opportunity to help the children pass by. "The Prophet ﷺ also said that a person who believes in and loves God ﷻ is not spiteful."

"What does 'spiteful' mean, Grandfather?"

"Layla, have you ever seen any children, or grown-ups, who are mean to other people? They even like to annoy, upset, and disappoint others?"

Layla exclaimed, "Yes, I have seen spiteful, mean children.

They upset and annoy their teachers, too. We children don't like spiteful people. I will be very careful to not be spiteful!"

Bilal added, "Sometimes I am a little mean to Layla. I won't let her join games with my friends and me. Maybe I should make an orange dot on my heart-drawing for my being mean sometimes, to remind me to be really kind to Layla and other children. Also, I don't like upsetting Father and Mother. It feels bad inside of me when I disappoint you. I am sorry that sometimes I am not kind."

Father Hamza said, "To say that you are sorry for a mistake and then to truly try not to repeat it is one of the best things you can do! It shows you have learned. I am proud of you!"

Bilal blushed and just drew an orange dot on his heart-drawing so he would not forget about how hurtful it can be to others when one is proud or spiteful.

The Book of Knowledge For Children

God ﷻ tells us that one of the most horrible things one can do is "back-biting."

Chapter 24
Back-Biting

Grandmother Aisha was extremely happy to see the children drawing their own hearts. A good way to be aware of things that harm one's special heart is to pretend each problem is a different colored dot. Like green for envy or orange for anger. While thinking about the spots that darken their heart's true brightness, the children added dots of color on their heart drawings whenever they thought about a problem to fix. They wanted to keep guard over their hearts and polish away the dots of dust. But first they had to better understand all the dangerous things that could cause their hearts to become dusty.

Grandfather Muhammad explained, "When you polish off a dot of dirty dust, it may keep coming back. But after a while, it will come less and less often and finally will go away. It will get tired of being wiped away and give up! If you practice not being proud or mean enough times, and even pretend you are always kind, one day you will discover that that's the way you *are*. You will have returned to living according to your pure heart and the dusty dots will be gone!"

Zainab asked, "Tell us, Grandmother, about more bad dust. What other dots should we be watching out for, the ones that keep on trying to get onto our clean, good hearts?"

"Well," said Grandmother, "do you ever hear children, and even parents, talking badly about someone who is not there?" She frowned.

"Yes, Grandmother, I do. I hear some girls saying bad things about a girl no one likes. Things that aren't even true!"

"This is called 'back-biting,' Zainab, because they are talking behind that little girl's back. She is not even there to tell them that what they are saying is wrong. What do you think you should do when you hear children talking badly about another child?"

"I should try to tell them good things about that child because everybody has good things! And if they won't listen to me, I will walk away and not join them."

"You are correct, my child, not to listen. Imam al-Ghazali says that we also must protect our hearing from bad talk. Otherwise, we are joining in!" Grandmother Aisha continued, "And what about the child who is left out, the one they are back-biting?"

"The best thing I could do would be to make friends with that little girl," said Layla. That way she would not be alone."

"That is a great solution, Layla. God ﷻ tells us that back-biting is one of the worse things ever. Do you ever do it, yourself? If so, put a big red dot on the heart you are drawing for yourself and label it. Then work hard on polishing that dot away. People often gossip behind the backs of others. They may not realize, or they may forget, that this is a terrible thing. To emphasize how horrible it is, Allah ﷻ said in the Quran that it is like eating somebody who has died! You would never want to do such a disgusting thing ever, would you? So put it at the top of your danger list! No back-biting or gossip allowed."

"No backbiting or gossip allowed, *ever*," the children repeated solemnly.

Imam al-Ghazali

When the dust on your heart is gone, it will be like a shining mirror, and reflect Allah's ﷻ Light completely and perfectly. If you hold up a mirror to the Light, have you seen what happens? Light pours off.

Chapter 25
Beware of Making Excuses, Bragging, Prying and Spying

Abdullah looked sad. "I want my heart-drawing to be clean and shiny, but there are so many things I need to be careful about, and we aren't even halfway through the ten dangers Grandmother mentioned. Will I ever be pure enough?"

Grandmother Aisha answered. "Don't worry Abdullah, in time it will become a habit for you to always be watching and correcting your lower self. Imam al-Ghazali spoke about many things we need to do in order to be shining and pure with God's ﷻ light. It is just as important for us to know what *not* to do. That is why we are learning about all these things that harm ourselves and others."

Grandfather Muhammad added. "How wise you are, children. How very wise you are to find out all the dangers, *now*, while you are young and have time to make a habit of clearing up these problems just as they begin! If you think about it, you can see that Allah ﷻ gives us life and our lives and our problems and even the very dots that tarnish our hearts, in order for us to polish these away and prepare for the Next World. You must know what they are, so you can polish them away or avoid them in the first place."

Layla asked, "Why does God ﷻ want us to polish off the dots?"

Grandmother explained, "When your heart has all the dust gone, it will be like a shining mirror, which can reflect God's ﷻ light completely and perfectly. If you hold up a mirror to the light, have you seen what happens? Light pours off the mirror or off anything shiny. Then you will be able to love God ﷻ with all your shiny heart, and reflect His light in all that you do."

"And," Bilal added, "we will be able to go up the steps, one by one, as the dots are polished away—up the steps to Heaven where we will understand *everything*!"

Grandfather Muhammad said, "It is wonderful that you are working on your hearts right now. Did you know that you are better than some grown-ups who don't even know they have dots on their hearts? When you clean your hearts, you are more grown up than they are. It is good to see that you each have drawn your hearts on paper to watch over carefully."

"All right," said Bilal, who smiled and felt like a very big boy. "Tell us more. There must be so many harmful dots to watch for! What are more dot problems that we need to watch out for and get rid of?"

Grandmother sighed. "Here's a big one. Allah ﷻ said, '*Do not justify yourselves. He knows very well who is pious* (God-fearing).' (Q 53:33). You don't have to make excuses all the time about why you do this or that, just to prove that you did the right thing. The way you *are* in your life, the correct way you do things—God ﷻ is aware and He knows this about you. So rather than point out to people why you do this or that, simply be a very fine person. That says it all!"

"Yes," added Zainab, "I like good children who don't tell everybody how great they are."

"Zainab, that is called bragging. We don't have to go around telling everybody how good we are. Do you like people who praise themselves all the time and show off in that way? No, you don't like that. Why? Because even if it's true, it's ugly to point it out to everyone. It is true, but ugly."

"Imam al-Ghazali himself said that 'ugly truth' is when somebody praises him or herself," said Grandmother. "When a person is debating and arguing sometimes, in order to win, that person may spy on the one that he or she is arguing with in order to find out hidden things in their lives to be used against them. The Quran tells us, 'O people who believe! Do not spy on each other.' So we should never do this. Don't peek into peoples' private, personal lives. Don't you let others know what you want them to know about you? Don't we all pick out what we wish to tell others about ourselves? We should kindly listen to what people say and not spy into their lives to find out things that can hurt them or embarrass them!"

Bilal said, "That's right, Grandmother. We should never, ever look for others people's faults. All of us have strong and weak things about us! I would hate it if someone kept a list of all my bad points and then used them against me by whispering to people!"

Layla added, "It's true, Bilal. I do this sometimes. I think in my head that you are sometimes mean to me, and that you leave a mess on the floor after you play, and other bad things. And I want to tell Mommy and Daddy how bad you are, all the bad things I can think of that I know, so maybe I spied on you! I am sorry that I do this. I really would hate it if you did that to me! I will quit spying on you and telling on you."

Grandfather said, "Layla, you are becoming a better person every day. Go wipe away the yellow dot from the heart you drew, now that you are determined never to do that again."

The Book of Knowledge For Children

When our friends are joyful, we join them in their happiness.

Chapter 26
Not Wanting the Best for Others

Grandmother Aisha watched Layla shining up her heart-drawing. She added, "And children, one thing you must really beware of is secretly *not* wanting the best for others. It is a part of envy to not want the best for someone else. It means you are jealous and you do not want them to have good things in their lives. That is a very dangerous way to act and feel because it just makes you a low person. Remember that God ﷻ has a plan for you, also. Good things are waiting to come into your life, too. You should always wish the best for others. That is part of having a pure heart."

Grandfather Muhammad said, "One thing that I think is really horrible is that sometimes people argue just to make someone else feel bad. They want to argue and win the argument so that the other person feels like a failure. Sometimes you may be secretly happy if someone else fails. But this is such a terrible way to treat others. Don't you want to see them shine, too? So before you argue in order to win an argument, you must ask yourself, 'Is this how I would want to be treated? Would I like this?' Have you ever felt happy or glad because someone else failed at something? Or have you ever felt sad when someone else succeeded and did very well?"

The children thought about it. Abdullah finally said, "Yes, I guess so. Especially when it's someone I don't like very much."

"Well, I know that happens to people, but really, the best thing we can hope for is that our brothers and sisters succeed! You need to be happy for their happiness and not envy them," said Grandfather.

"This may not be that easy to do, but really watch yourself. And when you treat others as you want to be treated, you are becoming your true, real, beautiful self. Is it your lower self (*al-nafs al-ammara bi-l-su*) or your real, beautiful self (*al-nafs al-mutma'inna*) that wants others not to do as well as you may be doing?" Grandmother asked. She promised to explain about the three selves at another time.

Bilal admitted, "It's really hard for me to want my friend to do better than me at school or during games."

Grandmother explained, "Muslims share their joy and sad times with each other. So the next time you are with friends and they tell you their good news, be happy for that good thing that happened to them and say *al-hamdulilah!* Wouldn't you want them to be happy for you if something wonderful happened to you as well? The same thing applies for times of hardship. If they are sad, try to be sympathetic and understand what they are feeling so that maybe you can help them! If you were in trouble or needed help, wouldn't you like your friends to be there for you? To listen to your problems and care for you? Remember we are all like a big family. When we finish talking why don't you play a game where you see how it feels when you play-act this out with each other."

The children asked, "Is there one problem that is worse than any of the others?"

Grandmother replied, "Remember when we spoke of the difference between pretending to be good instead of being really good? Well, let's look carefully at why this is so very terrible for our good hearts!"

The children took a deep breath. There was so much to learn. And this part was not easy. But they were all so deeply relieved to start being able to understand what life in this world was about. Many of their friends at school just played games and watched films because they didn't have any idea of what their lives were for. They could be doing *great*, and even fun, things with what simply happens day to day. Imagine if all children could learn to transform their problems and bad habits into pure, shining hearts! Imagine what the whole world would be like if everyone did this!

The Book of Knowledge For Children

The sad bird was no longer chirping or flying. The children noticed there was neither food nor water for the poor bird in the cage.

Chapter 27
Being Two-Faced: Hypocrisy

One day Layla and Bilal were playing with a kitten. They dressed it in clothes and put it in a baby carriage. The kitten did not enjoy this at all. He mewed and fussed, but the children ignored his pleas and continued to treat the cat as if it were a toy. A man was watching all of this and approached the children. "Poor kitten! Don't you hear it crying? It does not want to be treated this way." He began to recite religious sayings about treating animals well. The children thought, *What a good and pious man! We were being very selfish*! So they took the silly clothes off the kitten and let him go.

A few days later, the children walked past this man's back garden. There was a dog tied up and twisted in a rope. He was panting with thirst. Near the dog was a birdcage. The sad bird was no longer chirping or flying. The children noticed there was neither food nor water for the poor bird in the cage nor for the dog.

Layla and Bilal ran home and told their mother all that had happened.

"That's a terrible story!" said Zainab, who was a great lover of all animals.

"You haven't heard the worst part. That man was what is called a hypocrite," explained Mother Haajar.

"That's a hard word," said Abdullah. "What does 'hypocrite' mean?"

"A person who tells people to do things and doesn't even do them himself or herself has two faces. One appears good to those he or she meets, but in secret that person is a two-faced hypocrite and only pretends to be good."

Layla cried out, "Yes, Mommy! That man spoke beautiful words and gave us good advice. We thought he must be very good and very kind."

Bilal concluded, "Layla, this is a good lesson for us to keep in mind. We don't want to add onto our heart drawings specks of ugly dust for having two faces and tricking others!"

"That is right. We want to act and speak in one way and be good children. That man is so mean to his pets and only pretended to be a nice man who cares for animals."

"That is why," Haajar said, "that you are supposed to say and do the same things. We don't like people who pretend to be one thing and act in another way, do we? We need to be the same person for everyone."

Imam al-Ghazali

The Book of Knowledge For Children

We love peaceful people, not those who argue and fight all the time!

Chapter 28
More Problems with Arguing

"I remember one day when Abdullah and his friend Hisham taught me a great lesson about arguing," Zainab said.

"What happened?" Grandmother Aisha asked.

"Yes, Zainab, what are you talking about?" said Abdullah.

"One afternoon Abdullah got into an argument with his friend Hisham. Their voices got louder and louder. I could hear their quarreling and got worried it would turn into a fight."

"Oh yes, I remember that day," said Abdullah. "That was a big disagreement!"

"Anyway, Abdullah and Hisham were fighting very loudly. I could hardly tell what they were arguing about, but each of them kept repeating himself over and over again. Each one of them thought he was right. And then the neighbor next door, a very kindly old man, came over to the fence and said something that made them both stop."

"What did the neighbor say?" asked Grandmother. "I'm curious."

"He said, 'The Prophet ﷺ tells us that Allah ﷻ will build you a house in the Garden of Paradise if you give up quarreling and arguing, especially when you are in the wrong. And if you do this when you are in the right, God ﷻ will build that house for you in the highest part of the Heavenly Garden. In other words, never argue with anyone ever! If you feel like arguing, just let it go! Even if you are sure you are right about something.' Abdullah and Hisham were shocked."

"That's right," said Abdullah, "we have always heard people arguing. We notice that boys and girls, and older people as well, seem to disagree often. We see people in the street and everywhere else, too, upset and in heated debate. And here was this older man explaining that even giving up this quarreling was another way to climb the ladder or stairs, to take another step up to Paradise and being nearer to God ﷻ."

"I guess Hisham and Abdullah never thought about arguing in that way before," said Zainab. "They did not realize that they could *use* that chance to make their hearts brighter and shinier by just stopping their argument. We all get opportunities like that every day."

"It's hard to simply be quiet and not fight back. Maybe I will try it, too. It will feel good not to get upset and always struggle to be the right one," said Bilal.

Abdullah replied, "Right then I was telling Hisham that my bicycle is the best kind there is and Hisham said that his bike was better than mine. I wanted to win out and show him that mine was better than his, but now it seems silly to argue like that. He is my friend and even if he were not, I can see how embarrassing and silly it is to act like that. It's true. When I see other people arguing as we were, it is really awful to watch. I don't like people who do that! It seems very low for good people to do that."

Zainab added, "You're right. I don't like to be near people arguing and quarreling. It upsets me, and nobody needs to prove that he or she is better, or smarter than his or her friends and school mates or brothers and sisters! If I show off like that, it will actually not make people like me better. I don't like show-offs and know-it-alls!"

Imam al-Ghazali

Layla said, "This is a very good talk we are having. We can all feel the goodness in our hearts. We can keep and stay with that feeling inside. We should just stay out of quarrels, especially with our parents! Listen to the story the old man told, the story about how God ﷻ will build us a beautiful house in the Garden of Paradise if we stop arguing, even when we are *right*!"

"Being peaceful is the best way to be. And we get chances all day long to do this! That is what Imam al-Ghazali is teaching us," said Grandmother. "Think how much you upset your dear parents when they hear you fighting and arguing."

The children, on their very own, decided to make a change. For their shiny hearts, they said.

Grandmother Aisha concluded, "Imam al-Ghazali reminds us that everything we do in our lives matters. Every little thing matters. One thing is certain: At the end of our lives, we will stand before our Lord and He will know everything that we have done or tried to do! He will know all of our intentions, every secret of our hearts. Imam al-Ghazali wants us to understand this well so that we might be encouraged to turn every moment into a moment of beauty and love, a moment of *practicing* what we have learned. You, dear children, are so very blessed to be able to understand now at the very start of your lives how you can *use everything* that happens to you as an enjoyable way to polish your beautiful hearts. That's the kind of good that comes from learning with knowledgeable teachers like Imam al-Ghazali. It is like he is giving us all a great gift."

The Book of Knowledge For Children

What kind of person am I?

Chapter 29
A Question for You

The next day after school before the children headed home to see their grandparents again, they stopped by the secret meeting place to see if Haj Abdullah were there. Out from among the trees he appeared, just as if someone had called him. Everyone was there, everyone except Layla who was home with a cold.

"We will not have a lot of time for discussion today," said their dear friend and guide, "So let us review. Imam al-Ghazali says that among those people of learning there are three kinds. Let's look at the different kinds and ask ourselves in which group would we want to be.

"Group one: These are people who hurt and destroy themselves and others. They spend their lives simply wanting more things and talking about getting them. They waste their precious time chasing after these. In the process they are literally destroying themselves. They are not using what they have learned to help others or even themselves. They will never become their best, true selves. Now, children, what are you busy with? How do you want to spend your time? Will it mostly be just for games and fun or will you use some of it to help others and help yourself?"

When Qasim raised his hand for permission to speak, Haj Abdullah said, "I just want you to think about these questions today."

Qasim nodded with respect and lowered his hand.

"Group two: The people in *this* group help and save both

themselves and others. These can be both humble and educated people, like your teachers, parents, and grandparents who teach others how to polish their hearts and how to be near to Allah ﷻ, while doing the same for themselves. Can you think of some of the people you know who seem to do this, who are humble inside their hearts and live humbly even if they are blessed with wealth in the outside world? Is this the group you want to belong to?"

The children thought to themselves that Haj Abdullah seemed to fit into *this* group.

"Group three: The last group of people are those who help others but are hurting themselves very badly. These are the ones you learned about called two-faced hypocrites. They only pretend to be good and yet they pass along fine ideas and stories. They are like the man who told you to stop mistreating the kitten but then you found out he was mistreating his dog and canary! They encourage other people to do good but in secret they do not do these good things themselves. They want people to think well of them—to praise and admire them. What they want most is to be popular and for people to have a good opinion of them. Believe it or not, almost all people are in this group. Children, you need to be on special alert and guard against this in your own lives. It is one of the worst pieces of ugly dirt on the heart's shining mirror. Watch yourself carefully for this weakness. Imam al-Ghazali has written a lot about this in many of his books that you will read later.

"Do you remember in the life story of the great Imam al-Ghazali, that even he, with his wonderful heart and enormous learning, even *he*, suffered from this problem? Imam al-Ghazali became famous when very young from all his learning. People came from all over to hear him speak and to listen to his opinion.

"One day, you will remember, he noticed that he was telling people to be humble and yet he felt that inside of himself was pride and a pleasure in being famous. And he knew in his heart that his life was on the very edge of a kind of crumbling bank. He was about to miss doing, and being, all that he was teaching others! But Allah ﷻ loved him so much that He stopped his voice when he went out to teach a class one day. After this sign from God ﷻ, Imam al-Ghazali left his home and town and even got a job sweeping floors and cleaning a mosque. He was trying to polish off from his own heart the specks and dots of being proud and full of himself and enjoying fame. And after many years he became empty of these problems. He became peaceful and quiet and humble.

"Then he returned home to his wife and daughters, emptied of all but his love of Allah ﷻ and very wise. And during those years he wrote for you and for all of us forty books to show us how to polish our hearts. He explained what things *really* mean so that you can clearly understand how to practice your faith and to regain your own true, polished, shining heart!

"So I am sure you will want to belong to the middle group which helps people in need and teaches by being good and true examples.

"What a waste of our short human lives—to spend precious hours and time trying to impress a few people who will die soon enough anyway—instead of trying to please God ﷻ Who is forever and ever!

"Imam al-Ghazali is asking *you* this question: Which type of person are you? Are you in group one, two, or three? You are busy each day—for what or for whom really? Do you think

God ﷻ will want anything from you at all that is not done for Him alone? Who are you, finally, trying to please? Allah ﷻ wants our hearts to be polished so they shine, reflecting His light."

The children raised their hands to answer but Haj Abdullah waved them off. "Today you are to think about these questions. We'll have more discussion next time we meet." And then their noble teacher walked off among the surrounding trees and seemed to disappear right before their very eyes.

Imam al-Ghazali

The Book of Knowledge For Children

The Heart is like a house with angels living inside!

Chapter 30
Your Heart Is Like a House

When Abdullah, Zainab, and Bilal returned home, they saw Layla all wrapped up in a blanket on the sofa, drinking a hot lemonade with honey.

Haajar said, "Children, come! Your grandfather has come to visit, but this time without Grandmother. I know how much you enjoy his many stories. He is very wise and has been living a beautiful life from all he has learned. Maybe he can answer some of your very special questions that you have been having these days."

Zainab ran up and hugged her grandfather. The children always loved to see Grandfather Muhammad. He gave them some lovely gifts and everyone had tea and lemonade together. Later Grandfather asked the children, "What have you been learning lately? Anything interesting?"

The children did not mention their secret place and Haj Abdullah, but certainly had more questions.

Bilal replied, "Grandfather, we have been learning that *Real Learning* teaches us to polish our hearts and to look at our invisible thoughts, the ones you can't even see!!

"Oh, indeed," exclaimed Grandfather. "I remember from last week that you were all figuring out how to shine off the colored dust spots on your heart drawings. I can see you are being taught what is most important of all! Our Prophet ﷺ said, 'Religion is built on purification.' How very true."

"What does that mean?" asked Bilal.

Grandfather replied, "Purification means to make something clean, but not always just by washing it with water. So to begin with, cleaning, making pure, and polishing your hearts gives you the best base, or foundation. To build your life, or even a house, you need to build on a foundation that is clean and good—not ugly and full of holes and dirt. Imam al-Ghazali tells us that the heart is like a kind of house where angels come."

Layla cried out, "Angels live inside our hearts? What do they do?"

Grandfather continued, "Imam al-Ghazali explains that they bring the light of true learning from Allah ﷻ into our hearts. These angels are pure and holy and just, and they notice pure and good people."

Layla continued, "Are there things the angels don't like? Do they come to live in everyone's hearts?"

Grandfather explained, "Let's imagine your heart is like a house with angels living inside it, and you can feel their beautiful presence and guidance. Now, if you are, for example, angry and puffed up with pride, wanting what other people have instead of what God ﷻ has chosen for you—all these bad feelings would be just like frightening, barking dogs and all the angels would flee from your scary heart-home."

"Oh," said Bilal, "you mean that the specks and ugly dots of dust on our hearts, all the naughty thoughtless things we sometimes do, can be like barking dogs that scare away the angels?"

"Exactly, Bilal! If you are full of anger, or pride, or envy, it is just like having barking, mean dogs. The angels won't come. People build houses to live in, but the heart is like a house made by God ﷻ. Imam al-Ghazali explained that when an angel finds a heart empty of its own concerns, even for a brief moment, he settles in there."

"But Grandfather," insisted Abdullah, "how do we truly empty our hearts?"

Grandfather continued, "This is something you already are learning—how to polish your hearts! Polishing is the same as emptying or purifying them, isn't it?"

Zainab added, "I want to clean my heart-house till it sparkles and has no barking dogs. I want the angels to stay. I want to know the true, Real Learning that angels bring with them."

Grandfather Muhammad continued, "What you learn, True Knowledge, is not a question of how many new ideas and facts you are taught. It is *light* cast into the heart. Children, the story Imam al-Ghazali tells about the barking dogs is only to give you an example, using something you can see in *this* world as a 'metaphor' for deeper meanings that will be clear in the Next World."

The children fell silent. This was more than they could understand now, but they realized what a rich and meaningful universe Allah ﷻ had made and were thrilled to be on such a sacred and exciting journey.

The Book of Knowledge For Children

Pretend you are a brook or a stream, trying to carry your water to nourish a heavenly garden.

Chapter 31
Doing Too Many Things

Just then the front door burst open and in came Grandmother Aisha, practically buried in bags from the market. "I have brought all matter of cures for my dear, sick granddaughter Layla!" she cried.

Haajar smiled and took the bags from her mother's arms.

"We'll make my special soup and my special drink to make sure the child is well enough to go to school tomorrow!" Grandmother Aisha announced.

Poor Layla! thought Bilal. *Grandmother's special drinks taste awful—like the one made with licorice root! Yuk!*

"Well, we'd better get started!" said Haajar.

"You know all the recipes, dear," Grandmother Aisha said to her daughter. "Why don't you get them ready, and I'll just share some tea with the children and play a game! Besides, if we are doing many different things at once, we don't do any of them really well, do we?" Aisha winked at her daughter who disappeared into the kitchen to make the dreaded drink.

Grandmother settled right into storytelling mode. "Children, can you pretend you are a brook or a stream of water . . . wouldn't that be fun to do?"

The children imagined themselves flowing along, with the water rippling on their bodies. Fish beneath the surface tickled. This was fun!

"You wish to carry your water all the way to a beautiful heavenly garden, to nourish it. But as you flow along, some of your water gets soaked into the ground as you turn to do other inviting things, and some of you gets evaporated into the air. Oh dear, there is *not enough* water left to do what you wanted—to water and make your garden beautiful."

The children felt disheartened. They had wasted their water.

"Your time is just like that," Grandmother went on. "We are all given only a certain number of days and hours by Allah ﷻ and only He knows exactly how many. And He gives you this special time in this world to prepare to meet Him in Heaven. So you need this time to make yourself beautiful—to polish your heart—to water your garden! This doesn't mean you shouldn't have fun and play. It only means that you need to make certain that every day you are doing what you need to do to be your most beautiful self!"

Abdullah nodded. "We talked about this before, Grandmother! We need to make sure that every single day we don't *just* play but we do something, for God ﷻ! We can do something for God ﷻ every day. And every time we get rid of one of those dark spots, it's like pulling strangling weeds out of our gardens so our hearts can easily grow stronger."

Bilal added, "Yes. It seems like we have all the time we need to do these good things. We are children. But what *if* life goes by very fast and we put off making enough time to polish our hearts and learn real divine learning and do what pleases Allah ﷻ and our parents or teachers!"

"You don't want to run out of time, so you have to set up a plan now. Your daily prayer helps order your day!" Grandmother counseled. "Be careful not to fritter away your days!

One day you'll wake up and find you are suddenly an older person like me, and you will want to be glad that you have spent your precious life trying to be good and doing the right thing. I feel that way. But I have been trying a lot longer than you have!"

The children giggled. Grandmother Aisha was funny even when she did not try to be.

"And even though I have been trying a long time, it does not mean I can just stop. My heart needs shining continuously! We all need to be on guard against low thoughts."

As poor Layla drank the awful tasting drink and frowned with each sip, the children all burst out laughing. They knew Granny was right about *not* wasting time, but she certainly made horrible drinks to help children get well.

The Book of Knowledge For Children

What happens if you pour water in a glass that's already full?!

Chapter 32
The Teacher, the Lion, and the Jug of Water

Grandmother Aisha took another sip of her tea. "All right, I would like to ask you something. How is a teacher like the person who saves you from being attacked by a fierce lion who broke out of his cage?"

Bilal answered, "Is this a joke or a trick question?"

"No, it's not a trick or joke. This comes directly from Imam al-Ghazali's *Book of Knowledge*."

Layla, eager for an answer, exclaimed, "Please, do tell us how a teacher can be like someone who saves me from a scary lion!"

Abdullah and Zainab just looked confused.

"All right," said Grandmother, who enjoyed puzzles, "imagine you're at the zoo and suddenly a ferocious lion breaks its cage and jumps out on the path in front of you. If that lion attacks you, you're going to get hurt or maybe even killed. But if there were someone there who stopped that lion before he attacked, then that person has saved your life! Right?"

All the children agreed. That was pretty obvious.

Abdullah could see the connection in the trick question and added, "Our teachers and family and even others all give us learning and knowledge about how we can go to Paradise in the Next Life."

"Oh, I see!" cried Bilal. "What they are teaching us *saves* us! That special Real Learning saves us from wasting our lives and makes it possible for us to go to the Heavenly Garden! So that's how a teacher *saves* us—just like the person saving the man from being eaten up by the lion. The lion is dangerous just like being ignorant is dangerous. Knowing nothing really can eat us up alive!"

Grandmother was delighted to see how her question had led to so many fine conclusions.

Layla went on, "Yes, everyone! We ought to be nice and polite to our teachers and others who tell us true ideas about how we can be the best kind of shining children possible! We want to be saved from being dull children! There seem to be plenty of children like *that*!"

Then Grandmother asked everyone, "And do we only get these lessons from school?"

"No!" Zainab replied. "We learn from everything and everyone. The man being saved from the lion didn't care what kind of person was saving him, did he? He didn't care if that person were rich or poor, famous or unknown. And he thanked that person for saving his life."

Grandmother continued, "Yes! And we want to thank all the different people who teach us! They are all teaching us how to *save* ourselves, how to reach the safety of Paradise later on, and even now by being pure people. That is finally what is most important in our whole, entire lives! We need to be like dry land that is saved by receiving rain. Rain is like the teaching which is truly helping us to live."

Zainab added, "Grandmother Aisha is right! And since this special learning is very important, we ought to listen carefully! We can't go around thinking we know everything even though we sometimes pretend we do and we act like know-it-alls. We need to be open, quiet, and humble and listen carefully, so this learning can enter our hearts!"

"Let's imagine there's a glass full of water right here in the middle of a garden. Then Maryam comes in with a pitcher of water and starts pouring water into the glass. What happens next is that since the glass is already full to the brim, the water being poured in overflows all over the grass and is wasted! So let's pretend we are all empty glasses on the table. If we listen and are open to ideas and learning, when Grandfather and Grandmother tell us stories and give us good ideas, these can fill us. But if we think we are so smart and won't listen, all the really important lessons will be wasted on us. They will pour over us and fall all over the floor, and we will miss knowing about them," said Abdullah.

Everyone imagined that they were empty glasses. It was fun! They looked up and waited to see what was beginning to pour in.

Grandmother said, "Perfectly said, Abdullah. Now let's listen! And pay close attention! We need our hearts to be open and eager. Let's start right this minute. And aren't we blessed? And yes, let's pretend we are like the soft earth, ready to drink in all the rain that makes it possible for things to grow. Those who teach us are like nourishing rain. We need their help in order to live well and happily. So let's respect all the years of learning and experience our teachers and parents have. Let's be open like the soft earth and receive their ideas and stories like nourishing rain."

The children all lay down on the ground laughing, pretending to be dry earth in need of some rain. It felt funny to be dry dirt.

"What else did Imam al-Ghazali explain, Grandmother?" Layla asked.

"Al-Ghazali reminds us that we must not think that we are as smart as our teacher. Our teacher is like an ocean, while we are like little jugs. Our teacher is much stronger and more capable than we are. He or she can therefore learn things and discuss things that we are not yet ready for. When you are first learning how to swim, you stay in the shallow water, don't you? Only after you are really good at swimming and are strong, can you go into the deep part of the pool alone. Just because our teachers can swim in the deep sea all by themselves does not mean that we can do that right away. Learning anything is like this. While we are just beginners, we must not think that we are stronger and more able and more capable than we actually are. We need to take the helping hands of others to start."

Haajar called out, "Grandfather Muhammad and your father are home! Time for dinner!"

"We have all the time in the world to learn about Imam al-Ghazali," said Grandmother Aisha. "But for now, let's go in for supper!"

After helping Grandmother up, Abdullah and the rest of the children headed into the dining area to wash their hands and get ready for the evening meal, to be followed by the family praying the evening prayer together.

Grandmother thought to herself, *We are all teachers by what we do and are and yet we are all students. Imam al-Ghazali reminds us that the beginning of knowledge is silence, then attentive listening, then memorizing, then acting on what one has learned, and at last passing what we know on to others.*

As old as she was, there was still much more learning to do.

Imam al-Ghazali

The Book of Knowledge For Children

*It takes lots of practice to hit the center of the target—
and also to polish your heart!*

Chapter 33
When You Shoot an Arrow, You Need a Target

After dinner, the children's father, Hamza, set up a round target in the backyard. He gave each of his children some small bows and arrows so they could learn to shoot. He explained, "I am sure you have heard about people who lived a long time ago, who hunted in the forest for food. They were skilled hunters, quiet and precise. This has been true with people all over the world since ancient times. So I have decided to teach all of you how to shoot a bow with arrows. Also, our Prophet ﷺ used to say to his Companions, 'Teach your children swimming, archery, and horseback riding.' You children already know how to swim and you've done some horseback riding, so now I've decided to teach you how to shoot!"

The children were thrilled by this idea but also a little hesitant. "But Father," Layla said, "it looks really hard!"

Bilal remarked, "It takes lots of practice, Layla. I play football and because I practice a lot, I can hit the goal and win a lot of the time!"

Hamza continued, "What Bilal says is true. In order to hit the target and win, a person needs to practice regularly."

Right before the lesson, Hamza talked about all the things they needed to do. "First, have a target. We have that. All right. Second, make sure you hold the arrow straight and look along it toward the center of the target. Then you must pull back the string very slowly, without ever taking your eye off the target, and then let the arrow go. And if you were hunting, you'd say

Bismillah just at the moment the arrow flew."

Zainab said, "If reaching the goal and winning the prize takes practice, then it must be very similar to what Imam al-Ghazali is teaching us. He says that the real goal in our lives is not just about winning games but is about reaching Paradise! And in order to go there, we need to know and practice all the ways of arriving there, don't we?"

"Of course!" said Hamza. "Just as you need to know and practice all the ways to win a game or hit a goal, the same is true for our life journey. In order to reach the goal we need to learn about all the things God ﷻ has given us to do and then practice them well. And this practical learning and knowledge takes us on a straight way. It is a clear path on our journey to the Heavenly Garden. As we practice with all He has blessed us with, our hearts will begin to shine more and more. And in the end, you will get a special, special, *mystical* deep kind of knowing of Allah ﷻ."

Abdullah said, "Yes and that's what happened to Imam al-Ghazali himself, didn't it? Remember when he left teaching because he was full of pride and enjoyed being famous? And remember he traveled, and he was even the janitor, the person who cleaned mosques, and then how his heart then began to shine more and more?"

Zainab added, "Yes, he set about really polishing his heart from all the bad specks of dust, and when he succeeded, he won the goal! His heart was shining and full of light."

Hamza concluded, "And that's why we are learning from Imam al-Ghazali. His heart became pure and it was shining. He kindly wrote forty books for us to explain the beautiful meanings that are found in everything in our lives and religion.

He did that for us. Imagine that after he polished the specks and dots off of his own heart, he was able to see what is really true and then share that all with us! Aren't we blessed to have such a wonderful teacher who is showing us the way?"

"I wish we could just hear stories from Imam al-Ghazali all day instead of learning math and reading and writing," commented Abdullah.

Hamza answered, "It is important to learn things in the correct order. If a mother bird builds a nest, she puts the strong twigs at the bottom and builds on these. Otherwise the nest would be weak and the wind would blow it down. So when you start to learn, you need a strong, solid foundation upon which to build. In order to build an airplane to take you up into the sky, you need first to study math. Everything you study teaches you how to get nearer to what is next above it."

Hamza picked up a bow and put an arrow in it. "Yes, in order to read, you need to learn the letters first. Then you go up from there, to what is after letters, to words and then reading. In order to get near to God ﷻ in prayer, you first need to learn how to do *wudu'* correctly and how to do your prayers correctly."

"Oh, I see," said Zainab, "it's like the steps you told us about. In order to go up and up and up we have do each step properly. We can't just leap to the top."

"Exactly true," Hamza said.

Layla said, "Maybe someday I would like to be a doctor so I can help people. The first step up is to learn math and reading, isn't it?"

Father Hamza exclaimed happily, "What a good and noble idea to become a doctor in order to help others! And remember what I told you about aiming our arrows at the center of the target and hitting the goal? I said that the real, main goal of our learning is to get near to Allah ﷻ and His angels by becoming beautiful people on both the inside and outside. You may study to be a doctor when you grow up, but from now on, your daily practice will be watching your heart and being sure you try to polish off dusty dots before they grow too big. Imam al-Ghazali reminds us that we should not leave on a journey if we have no destination or place we want to arrive to in mind."

Abdullah laughed at the thought of putting on one's coat, getting into the family car, and driving away, headed nowhere in particular. An exact destination is, of course, needed.

Bilal added, "And also, Father, you told us that even though Imam al-Ghazali says that making our hearts shine is the most important thing ever to do, he also said that in order to do that, we need to study all the ways that help make that happen, like reading the Quran."

"And that is a target we can all aim at!" said Hamza, as he let the arrow go and it hit the center of the target. The children were impressed and wanted to learn to do this, too. So they each picked up a bow and arrow and waited for their turn.

Imam al-Ghazali

The Book of Knowledge For Children

Let's pretend we are a herd of camels going on a journey together! But what do we do about those rocks up ahead?

Chapter 34
The Camels Leave

One afternoon all the children of the neighborhood gathered in the backyard of Haajar and Hamza's home. Ahmad suggested that everyone put on costumes and make up a play.

Yusuf said, "Let's pretend we are a herd of camels going on a journey together!" All the children agreed that this was a great idea. They knocked at the kitchen door and asked Mother Haajar if she could let them borrow some old towels that could be used as saddles and saddlebags.

"We need to feed those camels," said Yusuf, "so please let us use some kitchen pots, too. We promise to take care of them." Mother agreed but worried about her pots.

Maryam added, "Let's line up and walk behind each other like a real camel caravan in the desert. Yusuf, will you be the lead camel and we can all follow you?"

Yusuf agreed but asked, "Where will I lead you? Just around the yard?"

"No!" everyone replied. "Let's pretend we are making a long trip or pilgrimage across the dangerous, hot desert in order to reach Mecca!"

Qasim added, "For a journey like this, we will also need to bring supplies and food so we don't die in the sands."

Amina agreed. "Let's all crawl over and drink plenty of water from the kitchen pots and also put some food, some grass, in our towel saddlebags!"

All the children laughed. It was so much fun drinking out of a kitchen pot like a camel, even though no one had a long neck!!

Grandfather Muhammad was sitting in the sun in his special chair, enjoying watching the children crawling in a line with towels over their backs and grass stuffed in their pockets. But the camels ran into difficulty as they left the grass and began to cross a rocky pebble driveway that hurt their knees.

Layla cried out, "We must keep going across the sharp rocks if we want to reach Mecca!"

Some of the camels started to give up. They stood up and shook off the grass and striped towels. Slowly, the children began to gather around Grandfather, who had a big jug of lemonade and a large plate of cookies as well as fruits. As the children ate their snack, Grandfather took the opportunity to tell them a camel story from Imam al-Ghazali.

"Children, the game you were just playing is like your journey through life. Instead of traveling on camels' bodies with their long legs and long necks, you are traveling in beautiful human bodies. Now, for the journey, all of you wisely prepared your camels!"

"Yes," cried out Bilal, "we gave our camels water and grass!"

"What do people need for their journey across life?" asked Yusuf.

"Well," answered Grandfather, "there are three things people need for this great journey called life. People need learning about *how* to make life's trip a real success. It comes in three parts."

Qasim inquired, "What are *these* three parts of learning?"

Grandfather continued, "First, just like you children fed your camels, you must take care of yourselves. You will want to study and learn how to do something that will give you a living. Maybe be a nurse or a teacher or a doctor. Also you need to keep your bodies healthy by eating the right food. That's like giving your camels water and grass, what they needed to prepare for the trip to Mecca."

"But we didn't make it!" cried Zainab. "The rocks hurt and we gave up!"

"Oh, my beloved children," replied Grandfather, "that is where the second part comes in. Once you fed your camels so they were strong and able-bodied for the journey, then there is a second part that needs your complete care and attention. When your camels reached the rocky road and ran into trouble, it's just like real camels crossing the dry sandy dessert. Now this second stage of your camel's trip, is like your very own pilgrimage but is an inner journey that you make inside of yourself, in your mind and thoughts. The rocky road and desert that you must cross to reach your goal are those specks of dirt on your heart-mirrors that need to be cleaned away!"

"Oh!" exclaimed Abdullah. "So the dots we have all been drawing on our heart-pictures and trying to polish away are like the rocks? If I don't help Mother and am selfish with my toys, if I envy what others have and am not pleased with what God ﷻ chose for me, if I whine and complain a lot, well, these are like the rocks, right?"

"Exactly!" Grandfather replied. "What a wise young man you are! You can see that what the rocks and desert symbolize are really the difficulties we all have in overcoming bad things in our character, things that simply need cleaning away."

Maryam, who had been very quiet, suddenly piped up, "So if we made maps of how to best cross the rocky desert, and learned about all the tiny things we would need to know about and take along on the pilgrimage, so if we learned all this and then didn't even *bother* to go on the trip at all, we would have wasted that learning, right?"

Grandmother was delighted. "Maryam has understood the true meanings! If you learn all the ways of clearing away the rocky spots from your shining hearts, and learn to recognize them, to really notice while it is happening that you are lazy, greedy, whining, selfish, envying—whatever your problem is—if you learn to watch these things inside yourselves just as they happen and then know how to start getting rid of them, if you *know* this and don't bother to do it, *then* you are wasting all this precious treasure trove of knowledge while you all simply sit around or play. This knowledge is of no use if you don't use it to get ready for the inner pilgrimage to reach your pure heart and real self!" she said.

Ahmad added, "It's like the story of the two wolves we heard! Do we feed the good one by doing good deeds and watching our hearts carefully? Or do we feed, or starve, the bad wolf that suggests we do naughty things?"

"*Ameen*! Let's starve the bad wolf!"

"The bad wolf is the part of you that is telling you not to even bother doing all the wonderful things you are being taught," said Grandfather.

"All right!" cried out Omar. "We want to go on *this* pilgrimage."

Abdullah said, "But first we want to learn how and then, afterward, go and not be afraid of difficulties or setbacks from rocks on the trail before us. We will take care of our bodies first—like feeding the camels, making preparations for this trip. Then second, we will set about cleaning up our hearts from the dust!"

Grandmother had come out into the backyard and had been listening. "Oh, children! How blessed you all are! I see you really do understand that if you didn't polish your hearts, you'd be just like those who spend all their time brushing and feeding their camels—your own bodies—while forgetting to even be on the journey to God ﷻ. The camels were given to the pilgrims to travel *on*. Your bodies were given to you to travel *in*. Your heart gets to ride inside your body, doesn't it?"

Yusuf asked, "So we travel in our bodies because they can carry us like camels on the life journey? What will we find when we reach the end of the trip?"

Grandmother explained, "Complete joy, rest, and happiness. No more problems, ever! It is peace, wellbeing, and nearness to God. Everything your heart most wants!"

"That's a lot to take in, I know," said Grandfather. "Especially for a bunch of camels. So maybe you should have some more snacks to make sure you are ready for the journey ahead of you."

The children all dug into the new batch of fresh cookies that Grandmother had just baked and brought out with her. They were sure they tasted much better than grass.

The Book of Knowledge For Children

Oh, Grandfather! Will you teach us some REAL, special Divine Learning?!

Chapter 35
Grandfather Explains Some Important Ideas That Seem Hard or Difficult to Understand at First

A beautiful wild goose flew down into the garden from the sky with her baby. The entire family and neighborhood children held their breath, watching as the baby goose copied every move made by its mother.

The children settled down and drank lemonade and ate goodies but kept an eye on the geese visitors in the backyard. Ibrahim said to the wise grandfather, "You have lived a long time and in your many years, you have learned a lot. We children can see by your presence, by your face and the way you are, that all that special Real Learning has made you peaceful and very kind. We, too, would like to be like you when we are older."

Maryam added, "Yes, Ahmad. But not all older people are like Grandfather. Many are even too busy to talk to their own little children and do not seem peaceful."

Ibrahim added, "Maybe those people are like the first group. Do you remember we were told that one kind of people learn many lessons and then don't bother to use them. Remember, they don't help themselves and they don't help others, because all they do all day is try to get more money and more things."

Maryam remembered and added, "Maybe one of the reasons we all love Grandfather is that he seems to be in the second group. He learned the beautiful and useful things God ﷻ teaches us in the Quran, and he tries to put them into practice and live by them. When we see that, we try to do as he does.

So he helps himself, he helps other people, and he helps *us*. We are trying to *copy* him, just like that baby goose is acting like a shadow to its mother—or is it a father?" Everyone smiled and watched.

Grandfather was very touched by the children's sweet words. He thought to himself, *Al-hamdulilah, God ﷻ has given me such wonderful children to be with in my old age!* Then, aloud, he said, "Really, wouldn't we all love to be part of that second group? The ones who learn and use their learning to help themselves and to help others?"

"Yes, I know I would," said Layla.

"Me, too," said Ibrahim.

"And me, too," added Maryam.

Grandfather interrupted. "Children, as you may remember, we all would love to be in the second group, but most all of us who have learned real knowledge and pass it on, do help others. But in as far as we don't do all the good things that Allah ﷻ and the Prophet ﷺ ask us to do, we are not saving our own selves. We need to try very, very hard to be as good as we can. Slowly but surely, those rocky dots you have all drawn on your paper hearts will melt away if you keep on guard and watch the thoughts as they come into your minds!"

"Thank you so much, Grandfather," Bilal went on, "for explaining this to us. We *need* to understand what life is for and why we were even born and what happens when we die."

Everyone sat in silence finishing their lemonades. Beautiful birds were chirping in the trees and sky, and the geese took flight while making their wonderful honking sound. As Layla watched them fly far off into the distance, she thought that all these ideas were not so easy to understand but she felt very, very glad that the children had people—grandparents, mothers, fathers, and teachers—who would help them learn and, over time, answer all their questions. After all, they had come to understand that learning is like going up step by step, slowly but surely, learning more along life's way. She was happy that Real Learning had steps to follow. And that Imam al-Ghazali had left a map to be followed by anyone who wanted to understand the real meaning of life on this earth.

The Book of Knowledge For Children

And Grandmother will tell you all about the three selves inside of us!

Chapter 36
The Three Selves

The children continued to sit quietly in the family's garden as evening fell. They wanted to hear more about their camel caravan game and what they could learn from it about their own lives.

Layla piped up, "Grandfather, we learned that when we prepared our camels for their journey by feeding them, that this is like our own lives. First, learn how to take care of our bodies that we are traveling inside of during our life's journey. Next we have to learn things that will later help us to find jobs so we can work and we will have money to buy food, clothes, and a home."

Qasim added, "Yes, Layla, but besides caring for our bodies, we must remember to always clean off the rocky spots from our hearts so that they can shine! Remember, when our pretend camels reached the rocks in the desert, we gave up! We can't give up! We need to look at those rock-like dots, which we draw to remind us of our selfishness, our laziness, our being unkind to each other! We need to prepare and fix our insides as well as our outside bodies to go through the life's journey correctly!"

"But I don't understand *why* we are getting ready for this trip. Why are we caring for both our bodies and also our hearts? What for, really?" Maryam asked.

Grandfather explained, "I am so proud you are trying to understand what life is *really* about. I will do my best to answer your questions. Even though the answers are still too difficult, too hard for you to completely understand everything, you will get some ideas you can use now and slowly add to—like building a castle from the bottom up! The reason you are first taking care of the day-to-day practical needs, like caring for your bodies as well as your hearts, is so you can go on the real journey, or pilgrimage, and learn mystical knowledge. Do you all know what mystical means?"

"I think so," said Ibrahim. "It sounds like mystery. So is it something mysterious?"

"Yes, that's almost it. It's the highest spiritual knowledge about things that are very, very special about Allah ﷻ, how to be very near to Him and His angels, and how He runs the world."

Zainab said, "I would give anything to know that kind of very special knowledge! We would love to know all about what God ﷻ and His angels are doing."

Grandfather smiled and was deeply pleased. "So children, when you finally are prepared and ready to learn this most excellent knowledge, it will bring you a kind of happiness that will be with you always in this world, and also in the next world. You will be able to understand the deepest and most beautiful ideas through your bright, shining, pure hearts. Another thing that Imam al-Ghazali teaches us in his books is about the three selves we all have inside us. Grandmother, would you like to tell these wonderful children about that?"

"*Bismillah*," began Grandmother, gazing at the children with the kindest smiling face. "So, dear ones, you are slowly becoming aware of many wonderful things and finding out more about divine learning. What is it, inside of each one of you, that loves and is attracted to this special learning? Can you guess what part of you is trying to become nearer to God ﷻ?"

"The spiritual heart!" exclaimed the children.

"Just as you guessed, it is the heart! You have been hearing a lot about the heart—the spiritual heart, not the one that pumps blood through your outer, physical body. When you cut your finger you see some of this blood, don't you? Remember how Imam al-Ghazali told you that this special, invisible heart is like a mirror reflecting back God's ﷻ light? And remember how he explained that the thoughtless and unkind things we do are like a layer of thick dust covering our secret heart-mirrors?"

"Yes!" exclaimed Bilal.

"That's what we need to clean off our hearts, those dirty spots," added Zainab. "But *how*?"

"Well, *al-hamdulilah*, our Prophet ﷺ told us *how*. Do you know what he said?"

The children were silent. They weren't quite sure what Grandmother was going to say. "He explained that our hearts can get tarnished, sort of like this brass tray." Grandmother pointed to the tray, holding the pitcher of lemonade. "Do you see? It's not really very shiny is it? But we can clean this with a little work. Some people use polish, but even just some lemon juice will do."

"Yes!" exclaimed Yusuf, "that's how we clean trays at home."

"Exactly!" went on Grandmother, pleased that the children were paying attention. "But for hearts, our Prophet ﷺ told us that the thing that makes them shiny again, the polish that takes away that tarnish is *dhikr*. This is remembering God ﷻ, repeating His names, and saying *Subhanallah, Al-hamdulilah,* or *La ilaha illa-Allah*. That's a way we can polish our hearts so that they can be beautiful mirrors again. And with that mirror we can see both outside of us and inside of us. Outside of us, we can see what is true and what is false, what is beautiful and not so beautiful. But what about inside of us?"

The children weren't sure what to say so they waited.

"It will help if I explain that we really have three selves, a false one that is low, one that is very high, and one that's kind of in between—the three selves that Allah ﷻ mentions in the Quran and that Imam al-Ghazali explains to us. So which shall we talk about first? The highest one or the lowest one?"

The children looked at each other and exchanged thoughts. Then Maryam said, "Can we know about the low one first, and then can we go up?"

"Good idea!" answered Grandmother. "The lowest one called *al-nafs al-ammara bi-l-su,* the self that commands us to do what is bad and urges us to do selfish things (Q 12:53). But praise God ﷻ, we have another self, the next one that is called in the Quran *al-nafs al-lawwama*, (Q 75:2) the soul that blames. It's the one that tries to give advice and correct the lowest self, even though that lower self doesn't want to listen.

"For example, sometimes your Mother calls you to get up for school. Your lowest not-so-nice self wants to stay in bed. Then your blaming-self says, 'Get up! Mommy is calling you!' But what happens then? That naughty and lazy lower self says, 'No, I'll just stay snuggled up in bed a while longer!' But guess who is watching that talking back and forth between your blaming and lower self?"

"We know!" said the children. "It's the higher one!"

"Right again," said Grandmother. "That's your Real True Self, *al-nafs al-mutma'inna (Q 89:27-8)*, the soul that is already at peace and always near Allah ﷻ. It is in that self, our real self, that we all want to return to Him at the end of our lives! We learn in order to be this self! This self is in God's ﷻ presence, peaceful and content. Don't think you are the lower self that is pretending to be the only you. Now your wonderful body is giving your special, secret heart and spirit a ride as it hurries to meet the King of kings, God ﷻ! It's the same as if a camel were carrying you on its back on the pilgrimage toward Allah ﷻ. Wouldn't you take good care of that camel? So you need to care for your body, too, don't you? You want to get there, don't you? Arrive safely to God ﷻ, the King of kings?"

Bilal commented, "This is amazing! I didn't know that there were *three* selves inside me!"

"More than amazing," added Zainab.

"Sometimes, when I am naughty, Mother gets very upset with me and tells me what a thoughtless little girl I am. After a while I get very sad because I know I am *truly* not bad. This explains *everything*! So when my parents or teachers are put out with me, they are not mad at my real self (the self that is peaceful and watches my other two selves). No! When they are angry, they are only upset with my low naughty self. That's the self that makes all the ugly dots I have on my heart-drawing that need cleaning away! So! That little naughty self that I have, which only thinks about me, me, me and what I want, that little low, false self is causing all my problems!" said Amina. She was usually very shy so this was a lot for her to share.

Ibrahim added excitedly, "But my real *true* self is *always* good. It is the heart, the mirror-heart that once it has been polished shines like the sun! That's me! The real me! That's what the life journey and pilgrimage is for: to get the false, naughty me to leave so only the real me shines through!"

"My goodness!" exclaimed Grandfather. "Ibrahim can now see why Allah ﷻ has given us, in the Quran and *hadith*, clear directions for how to clean away the little, not-so-very-nice low self!"

Ibrahim added, "It's like people who just spend all their time feeding and caring for themselves or their camels. If we aren't busy polishing our hearts, we could even forget to make this amazing trip or journey in our bodies and hearts and we would lose our way and get lost *forever*. We wouldn't even get *to be* our real selves. We need to be who we already are. We need to be who we really and truly are. We need to remember this and not ever forget!"

Grandfather concluded the extraordinary afternoon with the neighborhood children in the backyard with these words: "Children, can you imagine being given this treasure, that you were made to be human beings, and then given this precious time that is our lives, and then, after that, only spending it mostly on something like playing games or watching movies? Or something similarly small and pointless? What a loss! This is what happens when people spend all their time on details of the outer life, the bodily life. It is a waste of our precious and most valuable time! Once time is gone, it never, ever, comes back. Remember the three selves. Remember the heart. Playing is also wonderful and we *all* enjoy games. But while we are playing, isn't it also a chance to polish our hearts?"

Yusuf, who had been quiet for a long time, piped up, "Exactly. What we can do all day, no matter what we are doing, is to help our blaming self stop our lower self. When we see Mother needing help carrying in packages, and our lower selves think 'I will just stay here and not help,' when we notice that low thought, we must join with our blaming self and say firmly, 'Push right on through that lower thought! Help mother *now*!'"

The children all spoke at once.

"What fun!"

"We can do that!"

"We can keep an eye out for that dangerous, fake lower self!"

The Book of Knowledge For Children

You teach just by doing the right, correct thing because others will copy you.

Chapter 37
Getting Rich and Getting Knowledge

One afternoon at school, Ahmad told his friends that he had heard his uncle Mahmud say that a person could become rich in the same way that another person got real knowledge or Real Learning. Ahmad said that he found that confusing. Ali said, "Let's go and ask our teacher." So the children ran over and knocked on their teacher's classroom door where he was correcting papers. "Please tell us, sir," they asked him, "how gaining wealth and money can be like getting wisdom or Real Learning?"

Ustez Hossein replied, "The easiest way to explain this is to tell you what Imam al-Ghazali said in his *Book of Knowledge*."

"That would be great," exclaimed the boys. "We love how Imam al-Ghazali explains things. What did he say?"

Ustez Hossein started. "First, if you want either money or wise teaching, you then need to go out and find the place where it can be found, where it is. Secondly, think of how you can then get it. If you want to be rich, you will find a job or start a business and work very hard. If you want true knowledge (which is a treasure that you can never lose), you need to find wise teachers and also work very, very hard. Remember that the key to the treasure is asking questions. So that's how the two are alike: You need to find where to get what you want and then learn how to get it."

Layla added, "If I want a new doll, I can go to the store. That's where dolls are."

Bilal asked her, "But how will you buy the doll?"

Layla replied, "I will do little jobs for Mommy and save my money very carefully until I have enough to get the one I want."

Bilal said, "But remember, Layla, what we have been learning! Finally you always get tired of your new dolls. You even lose some of them after you worked and saved your money or begged Mother to buy the doll for you."

Layla said, "I see what you are really saying. Dolls and toys are fine but I do lose and break them. What our teachers explained to us is that if we get Real Learning, it can't be broken, ever, and we can never, ever lose it! It's ours forever and ever."

Bilal continued, "Exactly! And we know where to find it and how to get it!"

Layla added, "Yes, we find that special Real Learning with our teachers, grandparents, mothers, and fathers who learned from the Quran, *hadith,* and the Four Imams as well as other beautiful teachers like Imam al-Ghazali."

Bilal exclaimed, "Yes, we know where to find that very special learning and knowledge. And how we learn it for ourselves is by polishing the dust off our own hearts! By watching what we are thinking about, doing, and saying every day! And fixing it, if it's not good!"

Ustez Hossein said, "I think all of you understand how getting money to be rich in this world and getting true knowledge, so you will be rich in this world, and the next, are alike. You know where to find each and how to get them. But then what? A rich man enjoys spending his money that he worked hard to get, but then another possibility is that he really enjoys sharing it and giving it to others. Maybe he or she is able to build a hospital for the poor. Maybe the rich men and women have the blessing of helping those in need, like building schools or sending medicine to sick people."

Ibrahim asked, "But what about the person who has learning? How can she or he be like those generous rich people?"

Ustez Hossein explained, "Imam al-Ghazali tells us that the person who has learning and then shares this knowledge with others, these people are more noble than even the rich man who builds schools or donates medicine. When a person has this true special learning that polishes his or her heart, and then is able to share this by teaching it to others, *this* is the most noble and fine thing anyone can do. For while it is a blessed thing to build schools or donate medicine, we all know that the greatest treasure, the greatest gift in life, is heart knowledge, which can be used to help others discover their true selves and thereby enter the Garden!"

Ustez Hossein continued. "Imam al-Ghazali mentioned what our Prophet Jesus, peace be upon him, said, 'Those who know and then teach are called great in the Kingdom of Heaven.' The teacher is lit like the sun, which gives light to others, as well as to itself. Have you ever smelled musk or a sweet perfume? It smells good in itself and yet it gives off a lovely smell all around it, to everyone! Children, you can be, and are already teachers too, even now!"

Zainab questioned this. "But we are young. You have studied many years and are a teacher in a school. How can we teach?"

"You teach by example! Of course you can already teach and share what you have been learning as children. You teach just by doing the right, correct thing, because others will copy you. Give me some examples of what you have learned that you do and others can see. Others will see the light and goodness on your face and want to be as you are! They will see that you are happy and peaceful and they will wish to be that way too."

Layla piped up, "When Mommy tells me it is time for bed, I can do what she asks, happily."

Ahmad added, "I was given a large box of candy by my uncle. It will be fun to share this with everybody."

Ibrahim said, "I saw someone being mean to a little boy at school. I can be kind and be his friend!"

"You see," said the teacher, "you are already teachers, sharing what you have learned! This is the best thing you can do!"

Imam al-Ghazali

The Book of Knowledge For Children

We are all the children of Adam, full of secret, shining hearts! Imam al-Ghazali tells us that when we teach others, we must be very kind and treat our pupils as though they were our very own children!

Chapter 38
Being a Teacher

The children were glad they asked their questions to their teacher at school.

Ustez Hossein was not finished and added. "Imam al-Ghazali tells us that when we teach others, we must be very kind and treat our pupils as though they were our very own children. Our Prophet ﷺ himself said, 'Truly, my relationship to all of you is like being a father to a son.' Your own parents, just like the Prophet ﷺ, want to take care of you in this world and protect you, and help you to reach the next world easily and safely. They don't want you to be sad later in your life because you weren't ready and didn't have the real Divine Learning that you need for this. So like the Prophet ﷺ, your parents and teachers, you too, even now, need to be good examples. Be merciful, kind, and compassionate to everyone you meet."

Yusuf exclaimed, "So if our teachers are supposed to treat us all just as if we were their very own children, then all the children in my class, and everywhere, are like my real brothers and sisters."

The Ustez went on, "Yes, Yusuf. That is what the Imam tells us in the *Book of Knowledge*. We are all like true brothers and sisters. And just as we love and protect our own brothers and sisters at home, we should love all others in the same way. God ﷻ made us all, and we are all the children of Adam, full of secret, shining hearts! Let's all imagine that we are one family, everyone in the whole world! Because, in fact, we truly are." Everyone imagined this and it felt warm and wonderful.

Omar said, "We are agreed that we children all want to go to the same place. We want to have polished hearts so we can all travel to Paradise when it is time to enter the Next World."

Their teacher explained, "Children, you sadly will meet people who only want to be ahead of others in this world. So they will be greedy, full of pride and puffed up. They will brag and show off what they have because they think others will like them more and envy what they have. They are not shooting the arrows of their lives at the same goal as we are! We don't want to show off what we have. We want to teach and share any good that we are learning, since we are all trying to reach the same goal: pure polished hearts! We aren't racing to beat anyone else, are we?"

Layla commented, "No, we understand it is an honor to teach and share the good we are learning."

Bilal went on, "We are so lucky and blessed because we understand that everything we see in this world, that money, food, and things just are there to take care of our bodies. Our real selves and good hearts are riding inside these bodies while we get the true Real Learning. The real treasure in this world is knowledge, what we know, not stuff."

"Yes," added Qasim, "it's clear that all those who teach us true and Divine Learning only want to help us get near to Allah ﷻ and not waste our lives struggling against each other to own more or just to become a leader or a president."

"That's right," added Maryam, "we are having deep meanings explained to us about what the Quran says and what our life is for! We are learning about our Prophet ﷺ, about his life, and how he did things, and what he said!"

Zainab added, "And besides that, our teachers are teaching us about the Next World and how to get there. We now know that we children must notice all the bad dust on our true, beautiful hearts and polish those until they shine! And Imam al-Ghazali tells us exactly how to do this in the books he has written for us! We know *why* we were born into this world! We have been given bodies to use and travel inside for many years until we have had a chance to watch over and polish our hearts until they shine completely, and reflect God's ﷻ light."

The children all looked at their heart-drawings and wondered how long it would take them to be dot-free. Not forever, but not right away.

Abdullah said, "Let's go over and see what Omar is doing by that tree."

Everyone jumped up and ran.

The Book of Knowledge For Children

What kind of teacher are you?

Chapter 39
Playing School

They found that Omar was pretending to be a teacher while everyone else had to sit and listen. He gave each child a sheet of paper and a pencil, pretending the space around the tree was a classroom.

Omar said to everyone, "Be quiet, students, or I will give you a lot of homework. Bilal, you talk too much, so go to the back of the classroom."

"That's not a very nice way to speak to us, Omar," complained Maryam.

"We love the kind of teacher who isn't mean to his pupils. You didn't have to single out Bilal and point a finger at him and say he talks too much! Why couldn't you tell us a story, instead, about someone who is quiet that could illustrate why that is so special and wonderful?" Zainab offered.

Amina added, "It's better to tell a story that teaches us about not talking too much."

"It was rude the way you treated Bilal. It hurt his feelings!" Layla said.

"We prefer a story that is so lovely that it makes us all want to be quieter when we hear it!" added Qasim.

"You're right," said Omar." I was wrong to embarrass Bilal. The best way to teach someone is not to point out his or her weak or bad points. That humiliates and takes away respect. I was wrong! From now on, we will all try, when we pass along what we have learned, to be good examples and tell inspiring stories that truly can help others. And the story should be easy to understand. Why even bother to tell a story if it is too hard to understand? When I talk to my baby brother, Abdal Fattah, I need to speak to him in a way that *he* can understand."

"That's just good manners," added Zainab. "In Arabic the word is *adab*, so it's polite, *adab,* to talk to people in ways that are easy for them to understand. We don't like it if a teacher or anyone makes us feel like we are stupid, do we?"

"No, we don't!" responded Layla.

"We should never ever make another person feel stupid," said Amina. "We would hate it if someone did this to us."

Omar continued, "So I was not being a good teacher when I shook my finger at Bilal. It hurt him. We should never say things to each other that hurt or cause pain. That might cause somebody to give up and not try anymore!"

"How terrible!" said Layla. "And sometimes we do that, don't we? Whenever we do that, we have to put a big, ugly red dust-dot on our heart-mirror drawings until we can stop being so unkind!"

Once they all expressed their feelings and Omar had apologized, the class was ready to learn. Omar wanted to tell a story that could show, in a nice way, what a good teacher should be like and at the same time, show all of the children how they could be good teachers too, as they learned new and wonderful ways to be.

"Tell us a story!" said Abdullah.

"Yes, a good one!" said Bilal.

Imam al-Ghazali

"One with adventures and heroes," said Iman.

"One with good guys and bad guys," added Qasim.

"And don't forget good girls and bad girls!" said Layla.

"And one that has heart lessons, please?" asked Yusuf.

"I know just the place to start, students," said Omar. "There's a great story about two tree branches in Imam al-Ghazali's *Book of Knowledge for Children*. We'll start with that next."

The Book of Knowledge For Children

Do you keep the company of people who are like straight or twisted trees? What is your shadow like?

Chapter 40
The Two Trees

As Omar sat at the front of the class under a large, shady tree, he began to read. "Living in a golden field were two trees. One was tall and straight and it reached its branches up toward the sun. A younger tree grew nearby in its shadow. There was another tree that was crooked, bent over, and its straggly branches grasped at things on the dark, damp ground.

"When the sun rose each day, the straight tree had a straight shadow that went out from the bottom of its trunk. When people passed by and they saw the straight shadow, they exclaimed, 'This is the way we should be, too! This good, beautiful tree is showing us, teaching us, that if we are correct and beautiful, then what comes from us, our shadows, will also be straight and beautiful.'

"The shadow from the crooked tree at the edge of the forest was jagged and scary. Everyone remembered what Imam al-Ghazali had said: that the teacher who guides and teaches and the student who wants to learn what the teacher is passing on, are like a branch and its shadow. Is it possible for the shadow to be straight when the branch is crooked?"

Omar paused and then said, "What could this mean? If your teacher is not the same fine person as the things she or he teaches, you will also be crooked because you are a shadow or reflection copying him or her. So when you go about in your daily life, sharing the good that you have learned, you are like the shadow of that tall great tree and then your shadow, what you are sharing, will be good, too. But if you are naughty, like the crooked tree, others will copy that instead. Because they are copying your crooked self, what you will leave behind is people following and copying a bad and ugly example."

Qasim added, "So be the good hearted person that you would be happy if others copied. Wouldn't it make you sad to think that what you did made an ugly shadow? That the people who copied you turned out badly? You must be what you want all those around you to be like. Don't ask others to do the right thing when you don't. Allah ﷻ said, *Do you enjoin what is right upon others and forget yourselves?*" (Q 2:44)

Omar continued, "So it is important and a great responsibility for each of us to be the right kind of person that others will copy and imitate. Haven't we learned how to do things by watching how other people do them? Imagine! Others are copying us, too! So we need to be at our very, very best all the time. It's an important idea, isn't it? And remember, God ﷻ especially loves teachers! Whales and ants pray for them, even!"

Omar closed the book. "That's all for today. Hey, everyone, let's go back and try that camel game again and see if we can actually get started on our pilgrimage for real, this time. Who's with me?"

All the children got up and ran from the tree where Omar had been holding school. It was time to try out some of what they had learned.

After they had played the camel game, the children ran past the town's forgotten garden on their way home. They looked at one another. It had been awhile since they had been to their secret meeting place.

Qasim called out, "We haven't seen Haj Abdullah for many

days. Do you think he might possibly be inside the garden?"

The children were delighted to find him sitting peacefully. They ran up and greeted him with joy. He was deeply pleased to hear all they had been learning.

Everyone moved in as closely as they could. Softly, their smiling friend counseled. "Imam al-Ghazali suggests, my beloved children, that we sometimes imagine that we are alone in the starry universe with Allah ﷻ." The children closed their eyes and imagined being out among the stars. "And before each of us is the day when we will be accountable for what we have done with our lives. And then, he suggests that we think deeply on what will serve us each best in our lives. He warns us to leave off, abandon all else. So I hope that when you have choices to make, 'Shall I do this?' or 'Shall I do that?' You will ask yourselves, 'Which brings me closer to Allah ﷻ?' Then you will *know* what to do. Peace be upon you all."

Haj Abdullah gazed up into the evening sky. Stars were beginning to appear throughout the sky, surrounding a tiny crescent moon. Everyone sat silently together, completely full of joy and peace.

Index of Sources

Listed for each chapter are the page numbers found in Imam al-Ghazali's *Book of Knowledge* from which his metaphors, stories, and teachings were adapted for the young. These references will help mentors deepen their own understanding of the ideas presented in the children's books and workbooks. MH indicates that the source is al-Ghazali's *Marvels of the Heart*. The list is in no way exhaustive because many of the ideas were found literally throughout the entire source work.

A Word from the Publisher: 14, 30, 140-1

Chapter 1 Two Kinds of Learning: 9, 13, 21-2, 51, 131-3, 156

Chapter 2 Animals and People: 10, 28, 51, 156, 260, 268

Chapter 3 The Two Worlds: 5, 11, 51, 195

Chapter 4 How to Enter the Garden: 12, 51, 192

Chapter 5 Excellence of Learning: 14, 17, 26, 27, 51

Chapter 6 The Best Gift of All: 4-5. 12-14, 18-20, 22, 29, 169-170, 181, 190

Chapter 7 How Do You Stay Really Happy All the Time?: 17, 25, 29, 52-53, 131, 133, 192

Chapter 8 Pretend You Are a Tiny Seed: 25-26, 42, 53, 145

Chapter 9 The Three Necessary Things in This Life: 25-26, 36, 52, 95-96, 156-158, 193, 214, 222-223

Chapter 10 Sharing the Treasure: 156-157, 215, 222-223, 227, 257, 234, MH 7-8

Chapter 11 What Are Things You Must Learn: 25, 36, 52

Chapter 12 Where Do the Wonderful Things We Can Learn Come From?: 39, 41, 50, 82, 84, 110

Chapter 13 More About the Two Worlds: 14, 17, 27, 51, 143

Chapter 14 Two Kinds of Things You Can Learn: 50-55, 86, 110, 145-146, 150, MH 32-47, 39-40, 60-61, 103

Chapter 15 The Story of the Two Wolves: 223, MH 36

Chapter 16 Important Things You Cannot See: 10, 13, 21-22, 131-133

Chapter 17 More Ways to Make Your Heart Shine and The Four Imams: 25, 47, 49-54, 63, 71-75, 85, 93-95, 110, 125, 145-146, 149-150

Chapter 18 The Ant and the Pen: 81-82, 91-92, 212, 222-223

Chapter 19 A Little Boy Loses His Father's Horse: 91-2

Chapter 20 The Little Gardens Inside the Garden: 16, 94-96, 213,

Chapter 21 How Can You Watch Your Very Own Hearts?: 18, 48, 51-52, 108-110, MH 32-47, 39-40, 60-61, 103

Chapter 22 Envy: 52, 53, 92, 128-129, 253

Chapter 23 Having Pride and Being Spiteful: 36, 52-53, 68, 129-130

Chapter 24 Back-Biting: 46, 65, 130

Chapter 25 Beware of Making Excuses, Bragging, Prying and Spying: 49-50, 130-131

Chapter 26 Not Wanting the Best for Others: 125, 131-133

Chapter 27 Being Two-faced: Hypocrisy: 85-86, 92, 132, 173-5

Chapter 28 More Problems with Arguing: 69-70, 114-136, 127, 133,

Chapter 29 A Question for You: 85, 106-108, 137

Chapter 30 Your Heart Is Like a House: 139-140, 143

Chapter 31 Doing Too Many Things: 26, 36, 82-84, 95, 107, 110, 191

Chapter 32 The Teacher, the Lion, and the Jug of Water: 21-22, 143-145

Chapter 33 When You Shoot an Arrow: 145-146, 150-152, 183

Chapter 34 The Camels Leave: 153-158

Chapter 35 Grandfather Explains Some Important Ideas: 132, 137

Chapter 36 The Three Selves: MH 7-8, 32, 51

Chapter 37 Getting Rich and Getting Knowledge: 28-29

Chapter 38 Being a Teacher: 12, 14, 17-20, 21, 27-28, 29, 160-161, 169-170

Chapter 39 Playing School: 17, 20, 29, 114, 152, 161-162, 167, 169, 170-171

Chapter 40 The Two Trees: 17, 20, 29, 114, 152, 169

This publication was made possible through the generosity of international donors and through the support of a grant from the John Templeton Foundation. The opinions expressed in this publication are those of its authors and do not necessarily reflect the views of the John Templeton Foundation.

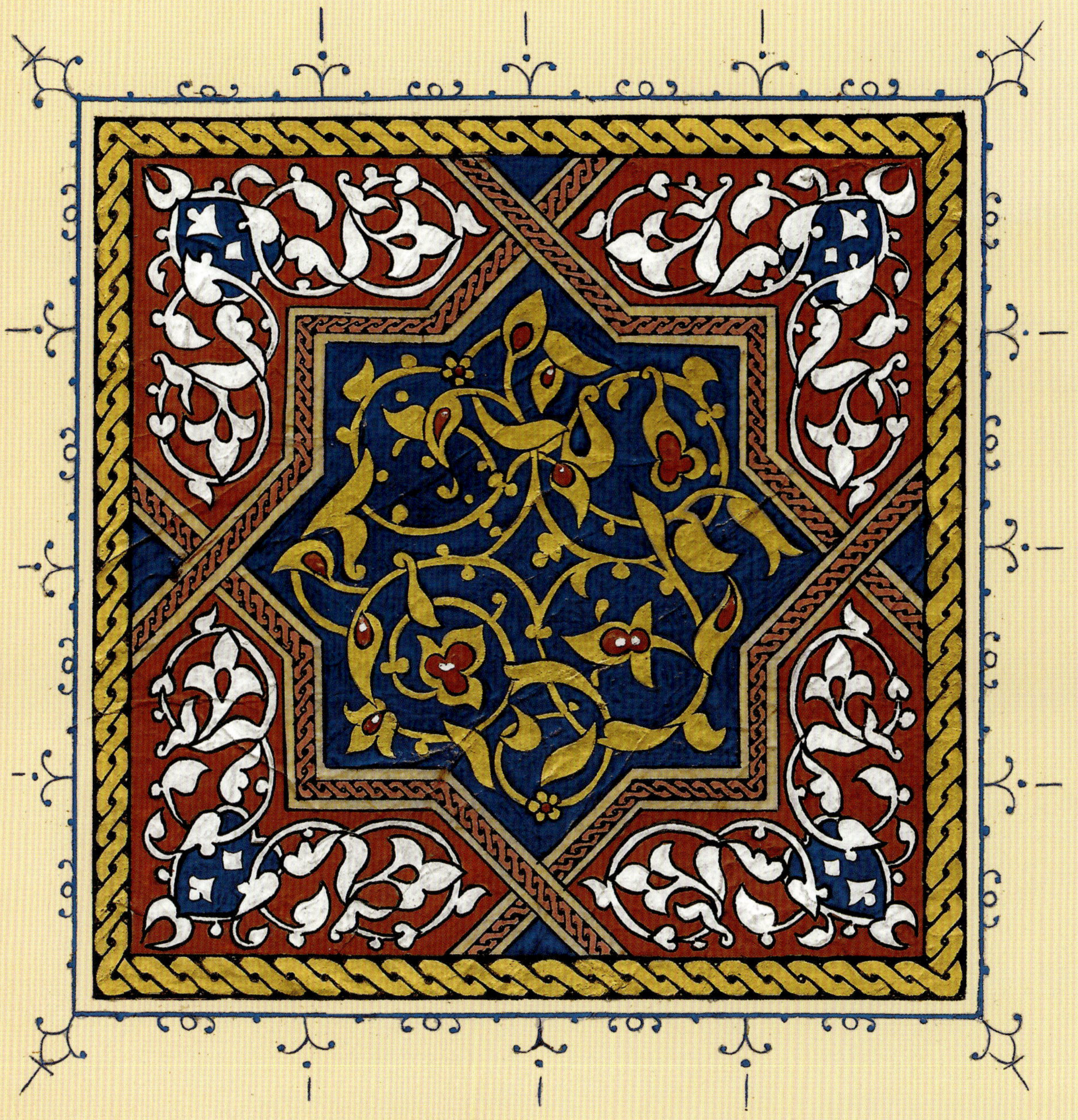

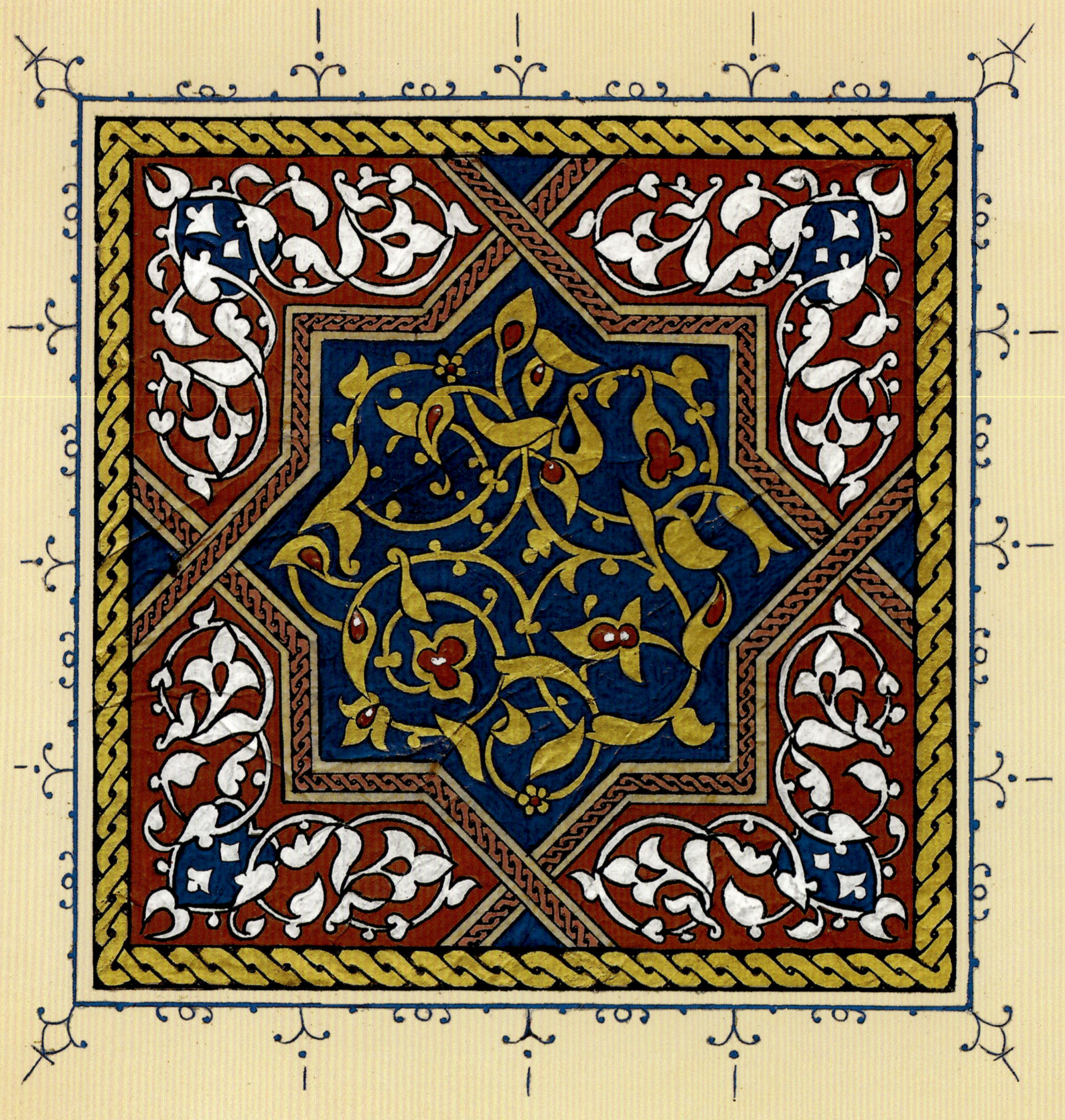